A DEVON GEM
The Bedford Hotel, Tavistock

ALEX METTLER

First published in Great Britain in 2013

Published by Philip Davies
The Bedford Hotel, Plymouth Road, Tavistock, Devon, PL19 8YG
01822 613221

www.bedford-hotel.co.uk

ISBN: 978-0-9576493-0-9

Design and layout
Roger Hayman

Printed and bound in Great Britain by
Berforts Information Press Ltd

For my darling Jane

who shared both my life and my love of English inns

Contents

Foreword

I feel honoured to have been asked to write the Foreword to Alex Mettler's work "A Devon Gem - The Bedford Hotel Tavistock". Having been the proud bearer of the name of Marchioness of Tavistock for 42 years the town has always held a special place in Robin's and my life and indeed our children too all feel connected to it. My eldest grandson, Henry, is now the Marquess of Tavistock.

Although, due to death duties in the 1950's, the family no longer have ownership of this beautiful town it will always feel like part of the Estate. When I was doing up the only house we still have in the area, I always stayed at the Bedford Hotel, Michael Healing was the Manager at the time, and it gave me the feeling of being "at home".

I found it so interesting to read this story and the part played by the Russell family. What an interesting life this grand hotel has had and how wonderful that its story has been so well recounted. I do hope that all who read it will do as the author has suggested and "Raise our glasses to the Bedford Hotel and the next 300 years."

Henrietta Bedford

March 2013

List of Illustrations

*The photographs from the Thorington Collection are reproduced by kind permission of the Tavistock and District Local History Society and Mrs Shirley Rose

Acknowledgements

I am indebted to many individuals who have encouraged me with their supporting enthusiasm in the preparation of this short history. The book is an extension of an earlier work published by myself in 1986 at a time of great change in my own life, a work that, for many reasons, was shorter than the subject deserved.

Thank you to all who have given freely of their time and resources, in particular James Bird, Stephanie Blanchard, Stuart Blaylock, John Bodman, Jane Brown, John Buckingham, Ian Carr, Andrew Chamings, Chris Chapman, Ann Cole, John Curno, Devon Record Office, Duke of Bedford and Trustees of the Bedford Estate, Hilary Davie, Kevin Dickens, Sally Dodd, Joanne Ellis, Mary Freeman, Barry Gamble, David Gee, Mrs Grylls, Lisa Hair, Dennis Harvey, Michael Healing, Trevor James, Ruth Lavers, Roderick Martin, Maggie McCall, Marion and Leslie Miles, Greg Mitchell, National Portrait Gallery, Mary Ovens, Pamela Parker, Keith Pendrill, Plymouth and West Devon Record Office, Plymouth Museum Image Service, RIBA Library Photographs Collection, Sharon Riggs, Chris Robinson, Shirley Rose, Simon Rowe, Tania Seldon, Lucy Shields, Jan Smallacombe, Caroline Lopez-Stephens, Willie Stephens, Sheila Stoneman, Rob Sullivan, Tavistock and District Local History, Tavistock Museum, Rosemary Wallace, Steven Whettem, Mervyn White, Gerald and Irene Williamson, Phoebe Woollcombe, Gerry Woodcock, and to Philip Davies of the Bedford Hotel for the publication of this book.

I also thank Henrietta, Dowager Duchess of Bedford, for her kindness in writing the Foreword. Henrietta is, and has been, a frequent visitor to the hotel.

Extracts from documents in the Bedford Archive are published by kind permission of the Duke of Bedford and the Trustees of the Bedford estate.

The layout and presentation of this book is, in no small measure, a result of the skills of Roger Hayman who has also demonstrated remarkable patience with the author when he was at times, being more than a mite unclear about his type set and image preferences and prone to occasionally leaving out little bits, which then needed correcting. Roger's skills and patience are much appreciated.

If I have left anybody out my apologies, it is not intentional but an aberration of my age or, perhaps, a result of spending too much time in the hotel bar.

The hotel has found and established its own place in the history of Tavistock and this work attempts to collect together facets from its history and to allow the reader (if there are any) to become more familiar with the hotel and its evolution from the ruins of Tavistock Abbey. This is not an academic work but is written simply because I like the hotel immensely and, since coming to Tavistock in 1976, have been interested in what, and who, shaped and formed the Bedford Hotel, and other hostelries, into the buildings and enterprises which we know today.

The work is my own and neither Philip Davies nor Warm Welcome Hotels have attempted to direct what should or should not be included and have helped with such hotel records that do exist today; it is indeed a pity that very few records concerning the running of the hotel have been kept or deposited in a safe haven, the more especially with regard to the lack of any extant Visitors' Books.

The responsibility for any errors is entirely mine and on receipt of notification of the same I will retire to the bar and chide myself unmercifully.

Alex Mettler

January 2013

The Bedford Hotel, Tavistock, in 2011

The Bedford Hotel, Tavistock

An Introduction

The town of Tavistock grew up around its Abbey that was built between the years 974 and 981 by Ordulf, brother-in-law of king Edgar. The abbey was badly insulted ie plundered and burnt to a cinder, in the year 997 by Danish invaders but rebuilt by Abbott Lyffing before the year 1027 and this monastic institution ruled the lives of the local populace with an authority unchallenged until the mid-sixteenth century. It grew to become the richest abbey in southwest England.

The rape of Tavistock by the Danes in 997

In the year 1539 the Abbey was surrendered in its entirety to Dr John Tregonwell, the Royal Commissioner and the property and lands passed to John Russell, the first Earl of Bedford. The abbey's riches were seized for the Crown, its abbot, John Penryn, pensioned off and, over subsequent years, the abbey buildings put to other uses or dismantled. Henry VIII was responsible for the dissolution of the monasteries and of the majority of his six wives. His father, Henry VII, had the audacity to introduce the first licensing statute for alehouses in 1495. Kill joy!

1

John Russell (1486-1555) was Lord Privy Seal in the reigns of Henry VIII, Edward VI and Mary, and, in 1539 was created Baron Russell and Knight of the Garter. The thirteenth Duke of Bedford in 1959, writing in his autobiography, wrote of Baron Russell

> "To combat the general unrest of the times a council had been set up for the West Country and Russell was appointed its president, more or less the King's Viceroy, with complete governmental power for the western counties. In order to increase his local standing as a landowner ... he received from the Crown the dissolved Abbey of St Mary and St Rumon in Tavistock. This made his income up to twelve hundred pounds a year, enormous in terms of the times ... "

John was granted letters patent on 4th July 1539 for "... the site of Tavistock Abbey and the greater part of its possessions ... " plus many other properties in the West Country, including the Scilly Isles. The decline of religious power in the area was thus replaced with a feudal landlord of immense wealth. In relation to Tavistock itself the power of the house of Bedford was to be exercised for nearly four hundred years.

John Russell, first Earl of Bedford, after Holbein the younger

In many areas throughout Britain the feudal landlord was to give his name to the principal hostelry in the area. This was so in Tavistock and the Duke's Arms, Bedford Arms, Bedford Inn and, latterly, the Bedford Hotel have all been used for the name of the town's principal inn over nearly 300 years. In addition the site of this inn throughout this period was centrally placed within the former abbey precincts and thus the inn itself has a truly fine pedigree.

As a country inn the Bedford Hotel has no great claim to fame and does not appear in any of the standard works on the fantastic legacy which the English public house has left in the mind of all who love the English inn and a pint – or three. What this hotel does afford is a story of an inn gently moulded into the history of Tavistock Abbey, the house of Bedford and, finally, public and private ownership. Its owners (leaseholders) over the period 1822 to 1955 demonstrate a web of inter-family relationships that are synonymous with a number of the best and largest hotels in Devon and elsewhere. The hotel itself stands large, obvious and proud on the main thoroughfare into Tavistock town centre opposite the parish church, waiting to welcome all for a good pint, fine wine, fine food and an ambience which both emphasises its history and, unlike many of its counterparts, it has married well its modern developments with the medieval.

The First Bedford Inn – 1719 to 1822

Prior to the dissolution the principal hospitality for the traveller was provided by the monasteries, such as Tavistock Abbey, and it was only after the dissolution 'that the inn really established itself as a national institution'. From the 18th century on wayside and small town inns could offer reasonable accommodation and dining facilities. Despite Tavistock being a relatively small town there were 28 Recognisances taken out by victuallers and alehouses keepers in 1753 but apart from the Bedford Arms and, possibly, the Turks Head (later the King's Arms) in Higher Market Street, it is doubtful whether many of these premises offered much in the way of accommodation – there is, however, a singular lack of documented evidence to work on.

At the dissolution of Tavistock Abbey in 1539 control of all the Abbey lands passed to the Russell family and for the next four hundred years little went on in the town without the knowledge and, mostly, the agreement of the town's patron.

The Bedford Estate Papers, Leases, show that a John Smith built stables west of the Higher Abbey Gate c1719 and that he set up an inn, the Duke's Arms, on the site of the "old kitching and chamber and little turret thereunto adjoyning" From surviving leases it seems reasonable to conclude that the Duke's Arms originated in a building(s) on this site west of the Higher Abbey Gate. John Smith's venture was, however, not successful, and the land was mortgaged to various persons after 1729 and eventually returned to ducal ownership. There is no mention of a Bedford Inn, by this or any other like name, in the 1726 Survey of the Duke of Bedford's Tavistock properties and it is distinctly probable that the Duke's Arms/Bedford Inn was not trading for a number of years following Smith's failure in business.

In a view of Tavistock Abbey from the west, by Samuel and Nathaniel Buck in 1769, there is no building to the west of the Higher Abbey Gate, but there is good cause to believe that the Bucks were somewhat selective in which structures they recorded and which they left out. The 1741 engraving of Tavistock by Delafontaine clearly shows the inn to the immediate west of, and adjoining, the Higher Abbey Gate (now known as Court Gate), the easternmost entry to the Abbey grounds. The inn did, however, exist under the name of the Duke's Arms by the next estate survey in 1745. An undated list of public houses in Tavistock names the Duke's Arms under mine host Thomas Babbidge. For the declared election expenses of the 4th Duke a receipt dated 27 January 1741 shows that Thomas Babbidge sold two hogsheads of cider drawn at the Lower House in the Churchyard plus a great quantity of food, including oranges and lemons.

A note, dated 1743, was added to the Bedford Steward's Survey of 1740 which states that there was a small refuge which leant against the west end of the Duke's Arms. It had previously been leased to the Hornabrook family as a Milk House but in 1743 was described as "a little alehouse

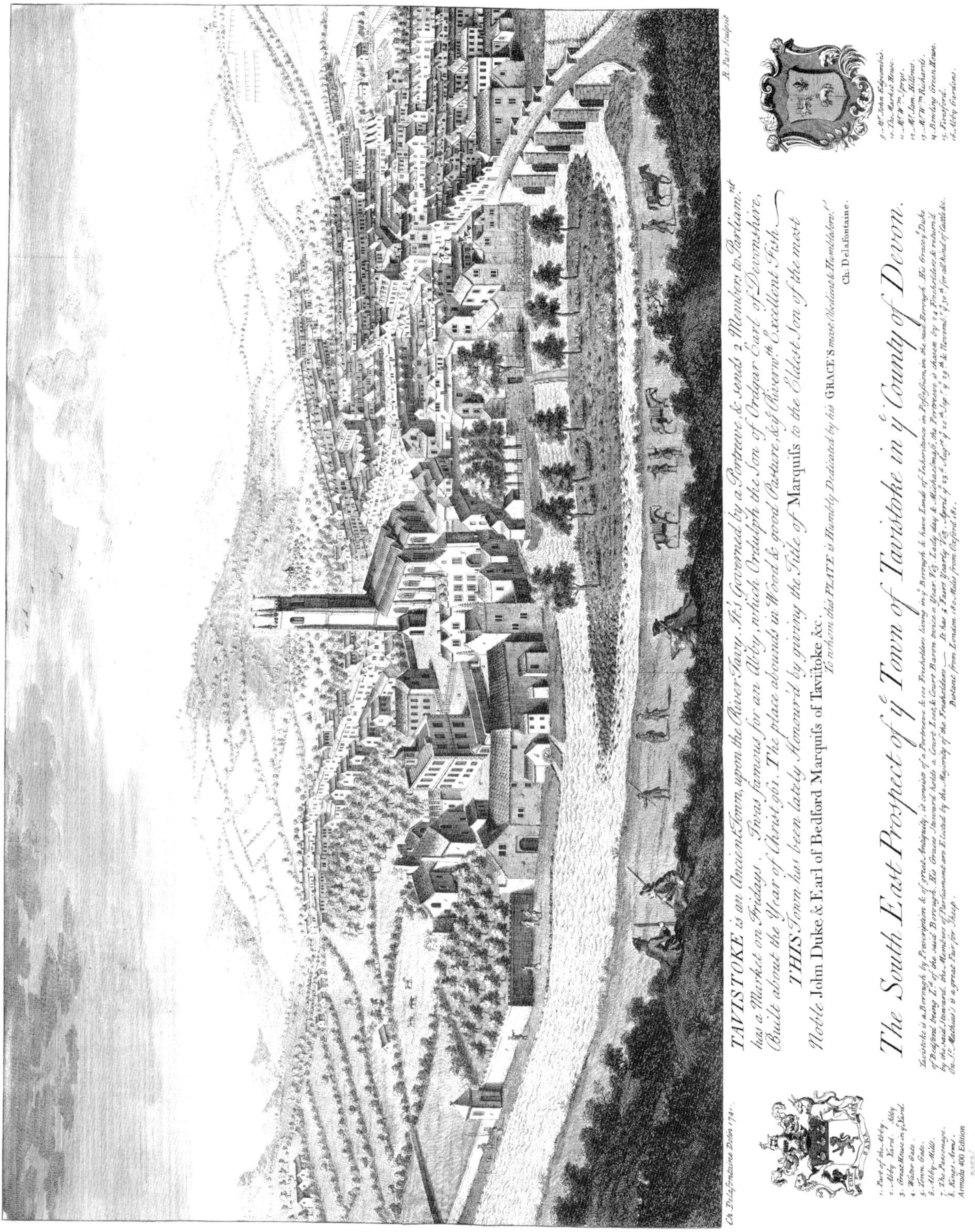

TAVISTOKE is an Ancient Town, upon the River Tavy. It's Governed by a Portreeve, & send 2 Members to Parliam.t has a Market on Fridays. It was famous for an Abby, which Ordulph the Son of Ordgar Earl of Devonshire, Built about the Year of Christ.961. The place abounds in Wood & good Pasture, & it's River.th Excellent Fish.—

THIS Town has been lately Honourd by giving the Title of Marquis to the Oldest Son of the most

Noble John Duke & Earl of Bedford Marquis of Tavistoke &c.

To whom this PLATE is Humbly Dedicated by his GRACE'S most Obedient & Humble Servant.

Ch. Delafontaine.

The South East Prospect of y.e Town of Tavistoke in y.e County of Devon.

Identification of buildings in the Delafontaine print

1	Part of the Abby	5	Town Gate
2	Abby Yard	6	Abby Mills
3	Great House in ye Abby Yard	7	Parsonage
4	Water Gate	8	Kings Arms

9	Mr John Edgcombe's	13	Mr Wm Richards
10	The Market House	14	Bowling Green House
11	Mr Wm Sprys	15	Fivesford
12	Mr Sam Hillows	16	Abby Garden

TAVISTOKE is an Ancient Town, upon the River Tavy. It's Governed by a Portreeve, & sends 2 Members to Parliamnt has a Market on Fridays. T'was famous for an Abby, which Ordulph the Son of Ordgar Earl of Devonshire Built about the Year of Christ 961. The place abounds in Wood & good Pasture, & ye River wth Excellent Fish.

THIS Town has been lately Honour'd by giving the Title of **Marquis** to the Eldest Son of the most Noble **John Duke & Earl of Bedford Marquis of Tavistoke &c**

To whom this PLATE is Humbly Dedicated by His GRACE'S most Obedient & Humble Servt Ch. Delafontaine

The Duke's Arms Inn, left of the Higher Abbey Gate (no 5), as shown in the Delafontaine print of 1741

and sells spirits this is a very little building but lying convenient for the poor people to drink without been seen … ". The mention of spirits being sold here is of interest, as although gin etc. was a problem in major cities of England at this time little appears to be documented about spirit sales in small country towns like Tavistock.

The rental papers of 1745 show the Duke's Arms to have at least 3 part tenants at will ie holders of a leasehold which could be terminated at any time by either tenant or landlord giving reasonable notice. The three tenants were Mrs Hicks at a rent of £5-0-0; Jonathan Bullen at a rent of £1-5-0 and Jno Hawkins with the stables part of the Duke's Arms at £1-0-0. By 1747 a William Skinner had become tenant, moving from the Fountain Inn in King Street.

The first documented record of the name of Bedford Inn appears to be in the John Wynne survey of 1752 that states "A house, Garden, Outhouses etc. called the Bedford Inn. Wm Skinner Tenant at Will who also rents the stable … ". A fuller description of the Bedford Inn is given by John Wynne in his Tavistock Survey of 1755

> "A large house, large curtilage, stable, brewhouse, keel alley and two gardens all contiguous on the west side of the Higher abbey gate, formerly called the Duke's Arms, now the Bedford Inn."

The site of the inn covered 36 poles (roughly 1090 sq yards) and commanded an annual rent of £23. Stables for horses were situated in the nearby Great Abbey Court (today's Guildhall Square). The keel alley referred to is a skittle alley.

The Bedford Inn, under William Skinner, enjoyed the direct patronage of the Bedford Estate and numerous written records still survive of expenses incurred by the estate at the principal inn in Tavistock during the middle years of the eighteenth century. For example John Wynne, the Duke's Steward, settled an account, for a dinner at the house of William Skinner on 14 February 1750, which reads as follows

	£	s	d
"ale and cyder before dinner for the wood buyers	0	5	4
to a dinner	1	0	0
at dinner, ale and cyder	0	6	8
samson	1	8	0
punch	0	7	6
coffey	0	2	6
wine	0	9	3
more ale and cyder	0	9	3
fire and tabacko	0	9	3
ale and cyder for the woodsmen at 1 shilling each man	1	17	0
	6	1	6"

Such affairs do appear to have been rather liquid.

In the eighteenth century seesaw legislation, relating to taxation on alcohol, licensing and the power of the local Justices of the Peace in relation to public house control, led to a massive increase in gin drinking. Although drunkenness due to relatively cheap gin was seen mainly in the larger cities, cheap gin and disorderly houses were to be found all over the country. In Tavistock, at the 1757 Annual Licensing Sessions representations were made to the Justices to deny a licence to William Skinner for selling spirits to the poor.

Thomas Salmon, Vicar of Tavistock, was incensed at William Skinner keeping a 'disorderly house' and that he, Skinner, sold gin and other spirits to the poor of Tavistock. Thomas teamed up with the 'churchwardens and principal inhabitants of the town' to teach Skinner a lesson which he may or may not have deserved. The representations to the Justices of the Peace on 1 September 1757 to refuse Skinner a licence do, however, contain complaints that Skinner's selling of gin was bad for the poor (who likely enjoyed cheap alcohol), was bad for the parish as the drunks would end up on Parish Relief and, additionally, prejudiced the 'ancient and accustomed inns which we are convinced are sufficient for the business of the town." The complainants were, however, Big Guns. Various groups wrote separately to the JP requesting that Skinner lose his licence, and presumably his living. The case of one representation reads –

"To the Worshipfull the Justices of the Peace acting in the Division of which Tavistock is a part.

We the Minister Churchwardens and principal inhabitants of the town of Tavistock do hereby request your Worships not to grant a Victualling Licence to William Skinner of the said town for the House he now lives in, as it must be a manifest prejudice to the ancient and accustomed inns of Tavistock aforesaid and of much worse consequence to the poorer sort of its inhabitants by the abuse he has already made thereof in selling at low rates great quantities of Gin and other common spirits whereby the poor have not only been frequently intoxicated themselves but in consequence thereof through disorder or idleness have with their families become chargeable to the Parish or been reduced to very great want, whereas such inconvenience have in a great measure ceased since he has been disabled from vending these liquors by retail

signed

John Tooker	Thos Salmon, Vicar	
Jonat Bligh	Peter Sleeman	) Church wardens
John Martin	Richd Vivian Willesford	)
Philip Harvey	John Wynne	
Richd Saunders	Richd Turner	
Richard Tooker		
Hu Crocker		
Nath Beard		
John Condy		
Andrew Beater		
Edmond Davy		
Pierce Edgcombe"		

Skinner lost his licence and was replaced by David Depear who advertised the demise of William Skinner with hand-written advertising bills which read

"Mr William Skinner late Tenant to His Grace the Duke of Bedford at the Great Inn in Tavistock lately known by the sign of the Bedford Inn but now of His Grace's Arms having been removed out of the same by His Grace's Order, the said Inn being now lett to me David Depear and intended to be forthwith fitted up in a Handsome manner. All Gentlemen, Ladies and others who shall be Pleased to honour me with their Custom may Depend upon Meeting with the best Accommodations and most Gratefull Usage from

> their most Obedient,
> and most Humble Servant,
> David Depear

Note: there are very good stables belonging to this Inn and the very best in the Town of Tavistock."

A part of the same notice from Depear also gives a short message over the name of Richard Turner, the Bedford Steward, which supplies confirmation that even the house of Bedford believed that William Skinner had been a naughty boy.

The tone of David Depear's advertisement was a rather smooth rebuff to William Skinner and

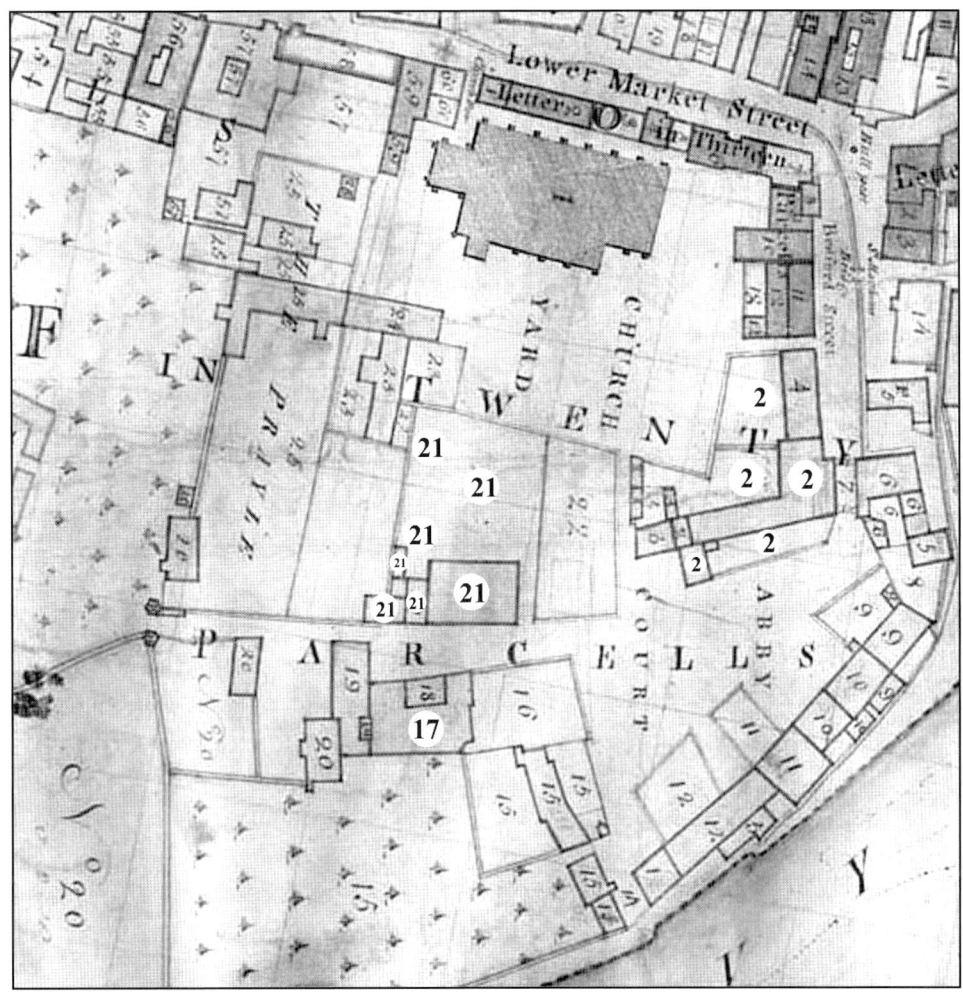

A section of the Wynne map of 1752 showing the Duke's Arms Inn (2), the Abbey House with associated out-buildings and gardens (21) and the present day Abbey Chapel (17)

framed in such a way as to curry favour with the Duke, from whose account Depear managed to borrow £400 to set himself up. Irrespective, Depear, in his turn, got his marching orders three years later. The reason for his removal is not very clear but there did appear to be some problems as outlined in a letter from Jonathan Jago on the 18 January 1760.

> "... I fear the poor man hath not been entirely blameless. Tho' 'tis said he will drink, I never heard that he was idle or drunken, but on the contrary remarkably diligent, active and tractable whenever company is in the house. The greatest, nay ye only fault I ever heard objected to him as an Innkeeper is in the badness of the cookery and the great indelicacy in providing entertainments, which of late, hath been so remarkable that I have been informed by ye Gentlemen of ye Militia that tho' they frequently desired him to be a little more careful in that particular, mere necessity obliged them against their will to leave his house as his meat in general was scarcely edible. "

*Notice from Richard Turner, Steward to the Duke, re the removal of William Skinner
from the Bedford Inn and installation of David Depear in 1762*

It is possible from surviving records of Depear's affairs, to calculate the approximate sales from the house in 1759. These were –

Dutch Genevre (Gin)	190 galls	Rum	154 galls
Port	145 galls	Madeira	12 galls
French Brandy	38 galls	Mountain Wine	38 galls
Lisbone	85 galls	Porter	128 galls
Beer	1800 galls		

Beer purchases were made of Hercules Pyne and only appear during the latter months of 1759 when Depear likely knew that his number was up and that he was due for dismissal. Nevertheless malt and hops continued to be purchased and the 1800 galls of beer is, in all probability, an underestimate of the total beer sold.

Gin and Rum were purchased from a Lewis Jones; port, madeira and porter from Michael Tanning and port, brandy and mountain wine from William Rowe. Michael Tanning appears to have provided bottles in hampers whereas all of Lewis Jones' deliveries were in bulk. Hercules Pyne, Henry Whitchurch and William Bunney all provided malt and Jones, Rowe and Bunney provided hops for Depear to brew his own beers on the premises.

The successor to David Depear was a Richard Morris who took over the inn in mid-December 1759. Despite some wrangling over monies owed for stock at the changeover Mr Morris was to be a landlord who found rather more favour from the Rev Jonathan Jago. The Bishop of Exeter made one of his Visitation tours, held four yearly, to include Tavistock in 1764. The Bishop's office requested of the Rev Jago advice on where best to stay in Tavistock and the Vicar replied

"The Bedford Inn is the most commodious house in this town, and at this House the Archdeacon's Court is constantly kept. The entertainment is, indeed, not always so good as could be wished, but on such an occasion I hope they will exert themselves properly. ...."

It would have been hoped that the 'entertainments' had improved somewhat since Depear's time but notwithstanding the Bishop's secretary appears satisfied with the suggestion of the Bedford Inn, with a request that it was most important that the rooms were dry and well-aired. Jago responds

> "Mr Richard Morris, landlord of the Bedford Inn promises to be very careful in the particulars you mention. The landlord tells me that they can make twelve good beds for gentlemen and about eight for servants."

The party ultimately consisted of six gentlemen, four servants and eleven horses. Suppers were charged at 1s each, plus wine, beer, cider, tea and coffee. The cost for the horses for stabling and feed was 14s 6d.

The Victuallers Recognisances for Tavistock show a Richard Morris as a tenant of a house (unnamed) from 1760 to 1764, which supports the above and a bill for £2 2s 0d against the Bedford Estate was paid to Richard Morris on 2 February 1761.

The Depear intrusion from 1757 to 1760, whilst not putting off the Bishop of Exeter, similarly

"To		£	s	d
11 pieces of beef	@ 12/- each	6	12	0
3 hams	@ 10/6 each	1	11	6
4 cheeks of bacon	@ 5/- each	1	0	0
10 dishes of fowls	@ 5/- each	2	10	0
7 geese	@ 4/- each	1	8	0
2 dishes of fish	@ 10/6 each	1	1	0
3 dishes of ducks	@ 4/- each	0	12	0
2 tongues and udder	@ 5/- each	0	10	0
2 calves heads hawk'd	@ 10/6 each	1	10	0
6 dishes of veal	@ 4/- each	1	4	0
2 candle pyes	@ 7/6 each	0	15	0
9 dishes of pease	@ 1/6 each	0	13	6
9 plumb puddings	@ 3/- each	1	7	0
7 rice puddings	@ 3/- each	1	1	0
8 apple pyes	@ 3/- each	1	4	0
roots and greens etc		2	2	0
		24	12	0
5 doz of red Port	@ 24/- dozen	6	0	0
11/2 doz of Mountain	@ 24/- dozen	1	16	0
3 galls of Jamaica Rum	@ 12/- gall	1	16	0
1 gall of Cognac and Brandy	@ 14/- gall	0	14	0
		10	6	0

Total cost for the dinner – £34 18s 0d"

did not seem to quell the appetite of the Duke's office for using the Bedford Arms for important events such as the dinner, on 11 July 1768, at the re-election of Richard Rigby Esq as MP for Tavistock. The bill is of interest, not only for the types of food served and the ratio of drink to food but also for the unit prices of the items

The above bill, made out by William Skinner, is also of importance in confirming the return of William as tenant of the Bedford from at least 1768. William was held under surety somewhere in Tavistock even in the years 1759 to 1764 when Depear and Morris in their turn held the Bedford Arms and had thus likely been biding his time awaiting an opportunity to return to this house.

William Skinner died in 1775 leaving a debt of seven and a half years of unpaid rent on the Bedford Arms totalling some £187, a debt still uncollected in 1781. The tenancy of the inn, and, perhaps, the debt, passed to his son, George Cumberland Skinner, who, like Depear, recognised the power of advertising. In *The Exeter Flying Post* of 31 March 1775 the irresistible virtues of the inn were revealed

> "GEORGE SKINNER
>
> Begs Leave to Acquaint the Nobility, Gentry and others that he has taken
>
> THE BEDFORD ARMS INN
>
> IN TAVISTOCK DEVON
>
> which has been greatly alter'd and render'd very commodious – He has laid in fresh stock of genuine WINES, BRANDY and other LIQUORS, for the accommodation of such Gentlemen etc as shall please to honour him with their commands, whose favours shall be gratefully acknowledg'd by
>
> Their oblig'd humble servant
>
> GEO SKINNER
>
> Tavistock
> March 27 1775
>
> The stables are also enlarged and greatly improv'd. Neat Post Chaises, Saddle Horses etc"

In 1783, in Bailey's Directory, the Bedford Arms was described as "a Good House". George Skinner would also appear to have kept good stables and in 1792 he advertised "To be sold without referee ten well-bred capital hunters and road horses, fast gallopers and good leapers".

During George Skinner's time at the Bedford Arms the hotel was visited by the Rev John Swete of Ashburton, a man who undertook extensive travels in Devon between 1789 and 1800 and recorded his experiences in sixteen written volumes. In 1792 he visited Tavistock and stayed in the Bedford Arms, which he found to a 'quiet haven' and 'a comfortable inn'.

At the close of the eighteenth century Tavistock town appears to have become rather dilapidated and Lipscombe, in his book 'Journey into Cornwall' in 1799, wrote

> "As we approached nearer Tavistock the country appeared rugged and disgusting. The town lies in a valley washed by the fine River Tavy, over which is a stone bridge. The streets are indifferently paved with a kind of pebble excessively hard and slippery. Many of the houses are of considerable antiquity and like old houses in general are dark, dismal and uncommodious.
>
> The principal Inn (which is the property of the Duke of Bedford) has arisen out of the ruins of the Abbey – the architecture of which is very evident in the building made use of as a stable. There is a fine arched gateway still remaining but the rooms over it are in a decayed condition."

The 'fine arched gateway' is the Higher Abbey Gate, the Court Gate of today, which is situated in Guildhall Square, and 'excessively hard and slippery' pebbles can still be seen in the immediate front of today's Bedford Hotel, down between the street facing railings and the front face of the building.

This period in Tavistock's history was to see the end of the Skinner's reign at the Bedford Arms. George Cumberland Skinner senr expired in 1802, "after a few days of illness", and in a short

The Higher Abbey Gate from the north with the Duke's Arms on the right – late C18

obituary in *The Exeter Flying Post*, he was described as ".. a strictly honest and truly benevolent man .. ". Tenancy of the inn passed to his wife Ann and during her tenancy moves were being considered by the Bedford estate to improve this part of Tavistock.

In an 1803 survey and valuation of the Duke's Tavistock properties the inn itself was described as " ... much out of repair ... " as were many other buildings in the town. In spite of this the rental for the inn had risen, from £20 a year in 1759 to £50 a year, and the inn must have been fairly successful to support such rental payment. Perhaps, however, all was not as it seemed, as the Skinners were not too good at paying the rent. At the time of his death in 1775 William owed seven and a half years' rental at £25 a year ie £187 10s, a very substantial sum of money at that time. These arrears were either written off or paid up later, but like father like son, George Skinner owed 5 years rental in 1786, a sum of £210. It needs be said that the Skinners were not alone in accrual of debt arrears and many other tenants seemingly thought that payment of rent was not for them. Things had improved for the Duke's rent collectors by 1789 when George's rent, still at £42 a year, was fully paid to date and this state of affairs continued until 1796 the rental being increased the following year to £50 a year, and paid promptly.

That the Duke's representatives were still not snappy enough to bring those in rent arrears to account, even half a century later than the time of the Skinners in the late eighteenth century, was a point noted by Denham, 1978, in his study of the Duke of Bedford's Devon Estate over the period 1820 to 1838. However, there is no doubt that considerable monies were being spent within Tavistock by the Bedfords to improve the built stock of the town.

According to a survey of the town in 1806 by William Bray, the Duke's Steward, " ... nothing can be done without a new structure from top to bottom ... " and with regard to the Bedford Inn Bray recommended that a new inn should be built on the same site

> " ... on the whole the site is most convenient and the yards and buildings occupied by the present Inn are of sufficient size to admit a building of magnitude enough to answer the resort especially as the stables and coach house are built apart between the miller's house and the Abbey bridge.

> It is very clear that in spite of the shocking accommodation the resort of strangers is increased and as there will soon be a great deal to excite curiosity that resort will need all computation if the accommodation is made good ... "

What Bray meant by " ... a great deal to excite curiosity ... " is unclear as the Duke's plans for revitalising the centre of Tavistock had yet to be formalised. It is possible that Bray was referring to the erection of Dartmoor Prison – work began in that year, 1806.

In furthering his idea to build the new inn on the same site, west of Higher Abbey Gate, Bray suggested to the Duke that the rebuild be carried out in two stages, demolishing half and rebuilding and then demolishing and rebuilding the second half. In this way the inn would not be totally out of commission during the alterations. Bray recommended to the Duke that rebuilding was to be at the Duke's expense in order that he could exercise control over the tenant, a control seemingly lacking to date if rent arrears are considered. In a letter to the Duke he states

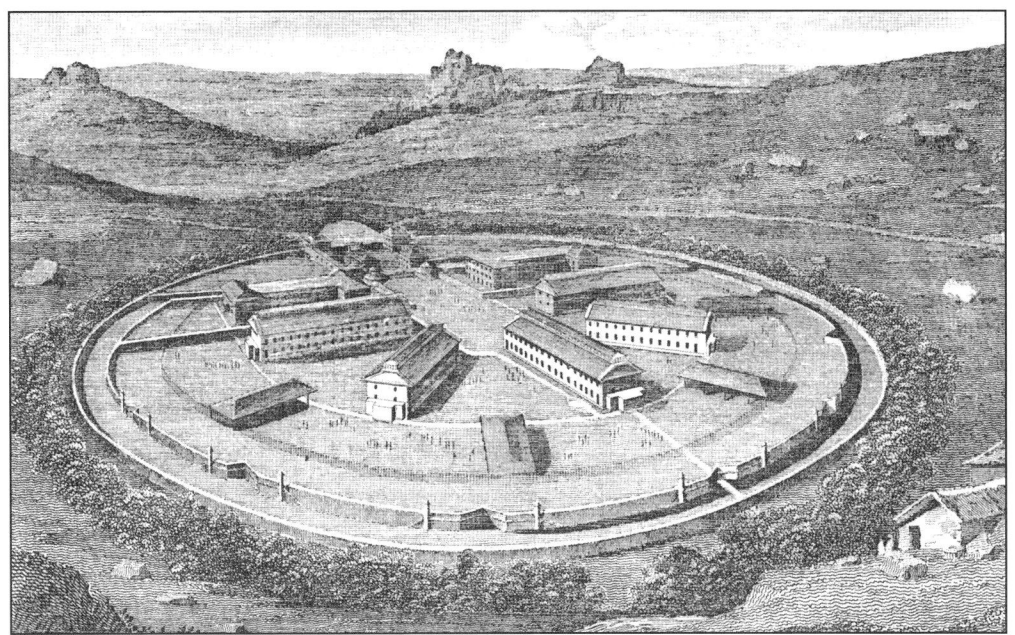

Prospective view of the War Prison on Dartmoor – after Charles Vancouver, 1808

" It keeps your Grace in that station of high respect and superiority so essential to the good gov't of Tavistock and prevents observations as to the Inn being built by subscription or tontine.

... If the people of the place choose to have a rival inn or tontine your Grace may then aid them with land for a fair consideration … It is the opinion of the best judges of Tavistock that the town can support a second inn."

At the time of the 1806 survey there were some 22 licensed premises in the town but none, with the possible exception of the Exeter Inn, in Lower King Street, or the King's Arms run by Thomas Prout in St Mathew Street, could provide the services of the Bedford Arms.

Despite its dilapidated condition the Bedford Arms was still used by the Duke for various official functions. Nevertheless, as with all matters concerned with the Bedford estate, expenditure was kept under strict control, even if collection of rents was not. Official functions were no exception as a letter in 1809 from the Duke's Steward of the day demonstrates.

"Presuming it would meet the Duke of Bedford's and your approbation to regulate and reduce the expenses of the Borough Court, I determined to begin the reformation of the Court on Saturday past when Boiled and Roasted Beef only was provided for Dinner, and in order that no imposition in Liquor should take place gave directions to two Innkeepers, Skinner and Prout, to bring their liquors to a room assigned to them for the purpose and after Dinner (to which only Freeholders, Tenants having paid their rents and the Borough Officers were invited) distributed tickets severally subscribed with my name of half a crown each, two to the Freeholders and one to all the others, to be spent on what they pleased, it produced the desired effect ... the room quitted before 8 o'clock and meat left given to the poor on Monday morning."

Doubtless the Freeholders and Tenants left grumbling that the boss had been a bit mean with the free drink but what effect, if any, exclusion from the party of those in rent arrears had in reducing such arrears is not known.

Despite the need for a second inn, and the apparent dilapidation of the Bedford Arms itself, the rebuilding of this inn was slow in coming. The Bedford Estate continued to use the services of the existing inn as shown by various expenses in the rentals and arrears books e.g. 6 July 1814 a bill of £34 14s 6d paid to Ann Skinner for a dinner to celebrate the Duke's birthday. In July 1814 the *Western Luminary* gave a report (published by the *Tavistock Gazette* in 1928) of Tavistock celebrations for the end of the Napoleonic wars. These celebrations coincided with another event, the Duke of Bedford's birthday

" The same day the freeholders of the borough dined at the Bedford Arms, in honour of the Duke of Bedford's birthday. This day was closed with a ball, which was well attended; the dancing was kept up until day-light warned the company to depart."

The Bedford Arms remained on the western side of the Higher Abbey Gate until 1821. In March of that year Ann Skinner died, aged 64, and it is clear that the decision on the future of the Bedford Arms had been made as the remaining stock of the inn was put up for sale. The inn was demolished and the materials sold to James K Colling, a builder and carpenter of Bedford Street, Tavistock. An added entry in the 1822/23 Rentals Book states that the three large stables and cow house associated with the Bedford Arms were "now thrown down and the ground cleaned for a cattle market"

A new Subscription Library – "a very fine room lighted from the top" – was built on the site of the old inn. Plans for a new library had begun with the death of William Tapson in 1819 necessitating a new home for the library stock that had been held in Tapson's Market Street premises since the founding of the library in 1799. Negotiations with the Duke's men to place the library in Court Gate failed and plans were drawn up for a new building and submitted for ducal approval, which was eventually given, despite some obvious reservations of the Duke himself.

With almost undue haste after the laying to rest of Ann Skinner in March 1821 work began on the new library, which was completed and opened on 1 July 1822. The building, nicknamed 'The Propylaeum', was designed, allegedly with Foulston influence, and built by local builder James Colling. The Library with a fine Doric portico, built for in excess of £1000, equivalent to some £40000 in money at 2011, was a prominent feature of the town when approaching from the west. It was, however, to be short-lived as the Duke did not like it, and if the Duke did not like anything of such a nature the odds on survival were short, or, more likely, nil. In 1832 the building was demolished and no trace remains today of either the old Bedford Arms or the library which replaced it. At his own expense the Duke refurbished the upper floor of the Higher Abbey Gate, known today as Court Gate, and built a library extension running east from the Gate, to include a Librarian's Cottage, known today as Court Gate Cottage.

South-west view of the Bedford Arms Inn, left of Higher Abbey Gate, after Coney 1820

*South-west view of the Higher Abbey Gate after the demolition of the Bedford Arms in 1822 and the building of
the mill (with turreted tower) but before the building of the Subscription Library in 1829 – after Allom 1830*

And of the Bedford Arms? The facilities of the best hotel in town were still to be provided by a Bedford Arms Hotel; whilst the old was being demolished and replaced by the library the new hotel was being completed from, and on, the site of the Abbey House within a stone's throw of the hotel's predecessor. Such was the timing that the opening of the new library was celebrated on the day of opening with a special dinner at the new Bedford Arms Hotel.

North view of Higher Abbey Gate c1853 showing the new Subscription Library, on the left, and Weights and Measures Office, on the right. The photograph was very likely taken by Tavistock photographer William Merrifield (the gentleman with the top hat on the right of the picture).

The Predecessor of the Bedford Hotel, The Abbey House – 1725 to 1822

At the dissolution of Tavistock Abbey in July 1539 orders were given to remove the Abbey valuables to London for the royal coffers and to generally sack the site. Although the Russell family were not to take over the Abbey properties for a few months yet, over the next 400 years the site was progressively plundered for building materials from the date of the dissolution. In 2012 parts of the old Abbey buildings are still to be found in many of the older buildings in Tavistock and in gardens within and without of the town.

A few larger, recognisable pieces of the Abbey buildings have survived, the best known and visually most obvious of these being the Still House, Betsy Grimbal's Tower (the western entrance to the Abbey site), the Higher Abbey Gate and the Abbot's Hall (the Abbey Chapel of today). The Bedford Hotel of today occupies the site of the frater, or refectory (monastic dining room) which legend refers to as the Saxon School.

Although there are a number of earlier references to a schoolhouse in the Abbey precincts, Woodcock in his study on the early history of Tavistock School, was unable to confirm that the presence of a Saxon School was anything other than legend. The existence of such a school, specialising in teaching in the old language, is best attributed to the discovery of two eleventh century anglo-saxon documents in the Abbey refectory building. Nevertheless, it is not until 1691 that the term Saxon School appears in extant documentary evidence. In that year the Duke of Bedford granted a lease to Thomas Willesford for

> " ... all that messuage of the dwelling house described as the Saxon School, the House or Great Room at the west-end thereof, and all the vaults and cellars underneath, the Room, Vault or House known by the name of the Dungeon, and with the garden or plot of ground on the North and East of the said school and premises with all their appurtenancies in the Great Yard commonly called or known by the name of the Abbey Court."

It is believed that Sir John Maynard, Serjeant, MP and lawyer, was born in the Saxon School in 1602 and it was following his death in 1690 that the lease of the property passed to Thomas Willesford. Maynard himself was something of an historian and made many transcripts of old documents relating to Devon and Cornwall, some of which survive today. In 1642, however, Maynard's house suffered attack by Cavaliers who " ... cut his beds in pieces, casting abroad the feathers, and pulled down part of the roof of his house."

On the death of Thomas Willesford we see real action in relation to what is now the Bedford Hotel. In 1712 his widow made over the remains of the lease of the Saxon School to Jacob

Saunders, a wealthy man owning considerable land in and around Tavistock. Saunders now proceeded to upset many in Tavistock by destroying certain Abbey remains and defiling ancient burial plots. The objective of his reported vandalism was to build himself a "pompous dwelling house" costing in excess of £3000, equivalent to some £250000 today. The Rev John Jago described the carnage in a letter to the Dean of Exeter c1750. He wrote

> "The Chapter House and cloisters were demolished by a worthless upstart of the town, who valued himself upon laying the foundation of a pompous dwelling house for himself and Family in the graves of the Abbots and Monks who lay interred in the Cloysters adjoining to the School and Chapter House, turning out their remaynes and stone coffins to publick view, with that inhumanity, Contempt and Ridicule of which non but such a wretch would be capable. But the event showed that he was only wasting his ill-gotten pelf in digging a grave for his short lived family."

In one of her many letters to Robert Southey, poet laureate, Mrs Bray states that 'In making the foundation for the Abbey House the workmen dug up, according to tradition, a stone coffin, or sarcophagus, containing the bones now deposited in the church, and called the giant's bones'. The sarcophagus removed in this venture is still to be seen in the porch of Betsy Grimbal's Tower, next to the hotel. The bones contained therein were two thighbones of great age and said to be those of a giant of a man some seven feet in height. Tradition has it that these bones are those of Ordulf, founder of the Abbey.

The reference by John Jago to Saunders' short-lived family is to the death of Jacob himself in 1725, before his house had been completed, and to that of his son John Cunningham Saunders

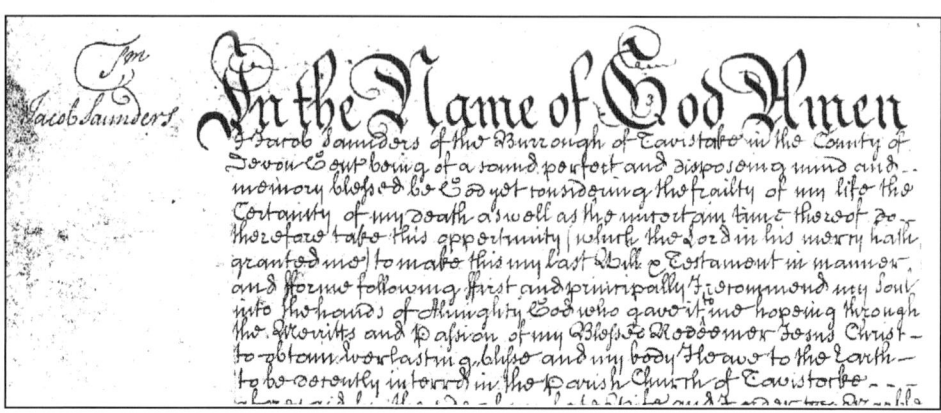

The opening part of Jacob Saunders's Will of 1725

The Will reads

*"In the Name of God Amen **I Jacob Saunders** of the Burrough of Tavistocke in the County of Devon Gent being of a sound perfect and disposeing mind and memory and memory blessed be God yet considering the frailty of my life the certainty of my death as well as the uncertain time thereof do therefore take this opportunity which the Lord in his mercy has granted me to make this my last Will & Testament in manner and fforme following. Ffirst and principally I recommend my soul into the hands of Almighty God who gave it to me hopeing through the Merritts and Passion of my Blessed Redeemer Jesus Christ to obtain Everlasting blisse and my body Heave to the Earth to be decently interrd in the Parish Church of Tavistocke ..."*

who died in 1752 aged 36. That the house was not yet built at the time of Jacob's death is confirmed from his Will charging his executors to finish the house and to obtain a new lease. This new house, when completed, was still known as the Saxon School and in 1726 a survey of the Duke of Bedford's properties in Tavistock refers to "all that Saxon School now a dwelling with a large courtyard before the said house, formerly a garden." The rent was £1 13s 4d per annum but a note in the survey entry states that "when finished will let for £20 above the rent."

The materials used for the construction of the Abbey House would indicate a dwelling erected by a man of means. Blaylock suggests that there is no evidence that confirms early views that this building was built on the foundations of older Abbey buildings and has described his findings of archaeological investigations in 1998 concerning the Abbey House as follows

"The exterior fabric of c1725 consists of high quality Hurdwick stone ashlar on a slightly projecting plinth just above the contemporary ground level ... The masonry ... is clearly of better quality on the north elevation than the south and thus identifies the north elevation as the principal one (as opposed, for instance, to the possibility that the building faced south in its original phase and was only turned round to face north later in the 18th century). The greater quality is represented in two ways: the facework is more rubbly on the side and rear elevations, and the plat bands marking the ground and first floor levels of the building vary in their materials. The ground floor plat band is of Beer stone on the north elevation ...but of Hurdwick stone on the side (E) and rear (S) elevations. The same distinction in materials is true of the plat band at first floor level, although it is wholly rendered on the east side, and thus could be of Beer stone; that on the rear is certainly of Hurdwick stone. Interior walls, everywhere the fabric is visible, are rubble rather than ashlar."

Jacob Saunders's Abbey House (marked 3 with the central cupola)
– from the Delafontaine print of 1741

There is also evidence that there were buildings to the west of Abbey House. However, Saunder's house, with its central roof cupola, which is clearly seen in the Delafontaine print of Tavistock town centre in 1741, does not clearly show any such buildings.

John Saunders had become heir to the Abbey House, with his stepmother, following the death of his father. On reaching his majority he bought out his stepmother's half share. On the death of John Saunders the Duke of Bedford bought back the lease for £100 in 1752 and some fourteen years later the Duke was to purchase all the remaining Tavistock properties that had passed to John Saunders's heirs. In this way the Duke added a further 21 freeholder votes to his already unassailable majority of 331 votes out of a Tavistock Borough total of 582.

It is probable that it was following the purchase, in 1752, of the lease by the Duke of the former so-called Saxon School that the house was re-named Abbey House. At the time of the Wynne Survey, given as February to July 1752, the house was in lease to a Henry Sanders (sic) and the Wynne Field Book of 1752 describes the property as

> "The Great House & Stable called the Saxon School a Large Court and Garden in Lease to Henry Sanders this was Bot ... by his Grace in Nov 1752 ... "

In the 1755 survey of Tavistock by John Wynne the house is described as

> " ... a large house, curtilage and garden before it with a stable, wash house etc, formerly called the Saxon School situated on south side of the churchyard."

The garden, which had previously been an orchard, had been added to the property in 1753.

The Abbey House was subsequently occupied by the Bedford Estate's Tavistock agents, who complained of the inconvenience of the house and its unpleasant situation so near the churchyard. The Duke's agents occupying the Abbey House included Edward Bray, a solicitor and the Duke's Borough Steward from 1775 until his death in 1816, followed by his brother William Bray who was the Steward until 1823. Edward Atkyns Bray, vicar of Tavistock from 1812 until his death in 1857 and husband of Mrs Bray the Victorian essayist, was born in the Abbey House on 18 December 1778.

It is not known whether the Abbey House deteriorated as did the general fabric of Tavistock during the later years of the eighteenth century, but the townscape certainly did not appear to have been in a rude and robust state by the turn of the century. In 1798 Gilpin had written, in a similar vein to the commentator Lipscombe the following year, that he was not impressed with the Abbey remains even though his knowledge of the original buildings was poor. He wrote

> "As to the Abbey, though it was once of mitred dignity and though, a considerable portion of it still remains, we did not observe a single passage that was worth our notice. What is left is worked up into barns, mills and dwelling houses. It may give the antiquarian pleasure to reverse all this metamorphosis; to trace back the stable to the Abbot's Lodge; the mill to the refectory; and the malthouse to the chapel:

but the picturesque eye is so far from looking at these deeds of economy under the eye of pleasure, that it passes by them with disclaim, as heterogeneous absurdities."

It was only some 5 years later that a survey of the Duke's properties in Tavistock noted that many buildings in the town were 'much out of repair'.

Three interesting pictorial records of the Abbey House and its predecessor are extant. A watercolour by John Prideaux in 1716 shows the old refectory, which the Abbey House replaced, in a somewhat dilapidated state prior to demolition; an engraving by Delafontaine in 1741 shows the newly erected Abbey House and in addition the survey map of John Wynne of 1752 clearly shows the site of the Abbey House and its juxtaposition within the Tavistock Abbey complex. In addition Finberg's reconstruction of the Tavistock Abbey site clearly shows the position of the frater and Chapter House sites where the Abbey House was built.

As the home of the Duke's most senior officer in Tavistock, the Bray's home would house functions of a political nature and in 1818 there is some evidence of this in that Lord John Russell's Ball was held here on 19 August, to commemorate Lord John Russell's election as MP for Tavistock borough.

Whether it had anything to do with the Abbey House becoming vacant or not the early nineteenth century was to see the Tavistock townscape receive an injection of monies to upgrade the Duke's properties in the town. In the early 1820s, as part of this upgrading, the "pompous dwelling house" was to be converted into what we now know as the Bedford Hotel. What also becomes more evident, nearly two centuries later, is that the buildings comprising the Abbey House and the later extensions of the hotel complex do incorporate parts of earlier stonework of the Abbey buildings themselves.

Tavistock Abbey in 1716 by Edmund Prideaux showing the old refectory (middle line 2nd left) that was replaced by the Abbey House

The Benedictine Abbey of Our Lady and St. Rumon at TAVISTOCK, founded c. 974, dissolved 1539, and here reconstructed in perspective

Reconstruction of Tavistock Abbey after Finberg 1969

1. The Abbey Church. 2. Monks' Cemetery. 3. Cornmill 4. River Tavy. 5. Water Gate and Abbey Bridge. 6. Still House. 7. Gardens and Fish Ponds. 8. The Abbot's Lodging? 9. Dortar? 10. Reredorter? 11. Infirmary. 12. Frater or Refectory. 13. Misericord.

Court Gate

The Great Court

Chapter House

Cloisters

The Prayle

The Parish Church of St. Eustace

26

The Bedford Hotel – 1822 to 1955

The fabric of Tavistock town was to see many changes in the early years of the nineteenth century under the eye and purse of John Russell, the sixth Duke of Bedford. Born in 1766, the son of Francis Russell and Elizabeth (nee Keppel) John succeeded his brother Francis, the fifth Duke of Bedford, who died a bachelor in 1802. John's succession to the dukedom offered him the opportunity to indulge in an extravagant lifestyle, spending lavishly on his properties and the finer things in life, including the building of a 'ferme orne' for his wife at Endsleigh, Milton Abbot. It was under the sixth duke that a new survey was made of the Tavistock estate in 1803 and thus started a long building programme of works that, under John Russell and his son and successor, Francis, the seventh Duke of Bedford, were largely to result in the present day Tavistock town centre.

Although the building known today as the Bedford Hotel was not opened until 1822 plans were being laid as early as 1816. In that year suggestions were being made that the then Abbey House should become the vicarage, the incumbent of the time having previously been housed in the area near the old East Bridge which was situated midway between the present Abbey Bridge and Vigo Bridge and demolished in 1762. William Bray, the Duke's Borough Steward and uncle of the then vicar Edward Atkyns Bray, was having none of it and in a letter dated 24 October 1816 he wrote thus to William Adam, the Duke's Chief Officer in London

> "As there has never been any regular vicarage house I see no utility in my paying the rates and taxes of the present nominal one, particularly as the sooner it is pulled down and the site thrown in to the churchyard the better ... I am not sure that my moderate income can keep it open ... It would be expedient ... to reside in it temporarily as a Vicarage House."

Correspondence on the subject continued and in January 1817 Bray himself again suggested that the Abbey House be converted to an inn, an idea previously suggested by him in 1806

> "I have strong reason for not wishing to take part of the Abbey House, which is this. Our families would be too near and Edward being very particular would prevent our going on with much comfort in such close contact. Depend upon it the best and most useful purpose you can convert it into is an Inn and I think it might be done without adding another story by merely raising the roof of the west end so as to be even with the other part."

The Edward mentioned here in 1817 is his nephew Edward Atkyns Bray (1778-1857), the vicar of the day, whose wife Anna (1790-1883), the Victorian essayist, was to write so informatively about both contemporary and historical happenings in Tavistock.

The above letter of early 1817 is most interesting as it implies that an extension to the west of Saunder's Abbey House was added after 1726. The Delafontaine engraving of 1741 shows a rectangular building of three storeys high along its whole length east to west. Bray, in his letter, describes a building with an addition to the west end and the presence of such is confirmed by the 1752 Wynne map where buildings do exist west of the main body of the Abbey House,

Contrary to William Bray's ideas, Andrew Wilson, the Duke's Land Steward, soon to take over from William, believed that the Abbey House was best suited to a future life as a vicarage and that to convert to an inn was not a sensible option. Some two years after William's letter in 1817, in May 1819, Wilson wrote to Adam –

> " ... The Abbey House is not suitable ... and unless completely gutted it could not be made at all convenient and even then it would not be a commodious Inn. It would be better to rebuild at once. But with submission I beg to suggest that I think it would be still better to abandon the idea of converting the Abbey House into an Inn and to adopt that of rebuilding the present Bedford Arms."

In his reply, by return of post, Adam stated:

> "I very much agree with you ... as to the Inn and almost hoped that the Abbey House was to be kept for the Vicar and the expense of his new house laid out on the New Inn in place of the Bedford Arms. But it is too late to think of that now even if it is right. But think over the subject well and converse with the Duke when he arrives ... "

The vicar's house referred to was the new vicarage to be built in grounds next door to the Abbey House and close to Betsy Grimbal's Tower. It seems clear that the decision had already been made, probably by the Duke himself, and that work had already started on the new vicarage. By August 1819 the Abbey House was empty and the vicarage built, and Wilson wrote

> "As the Abbey House will soon be at liberty and it being practicable to convert the

Edward Atkyns Bray

Mrs Anna Bray

The 7th Duke of Bedford from a portrait in Tavistock Town Hall

The 6th Duke of Bedford from a portrait in Tavistock Town Hall

same into a commodious Inn, I should therefore recommend that it be put into a complete state and ready to occupy before the Old Inn is done away."

These plans to upgrade the status of the Bedford Arms were undertaken simultaneously with plans to upgrade the then second inn, the Exeter Inn in Lower Back St, with the subsequent demolition of the nearby King's Arms in order to occupy the space between Higher Market Street and Lower Back Street. The demolition of the King's Arms would result in the creation of the Bank Square of today, a space that was to allow expansion of the market trading area of the old medieval commercial Tavistock. William Bray's plan of 1806, to have a 'second inn' was thus to come about.

By the end of 1819, the site of the new inn having been finalised, Bray now turned his attention to ensuring that the tradesmen of Tavistock were to benefit from the new development. On 25 December 1819 (it must have been preying on his mind to write on Christmas Day) Bray wrote to Adam

> " ... I refer to the New Inn. I think it would be but fair to confine the contract to Tavistock otherwise a number of workmen from Plymouth and other places might be introduced to the injury of the poor mechanics of this town, many of whom are out of employ. In addition to which the inhabitants of the town would also have a greater interest in doing their work well."

By the end of 1820 the work on the Abbey House conversion was well in hand with the object of completion in time for the Annual Licensing Sessions in September 1821. The prospective tenant had been identified as John Truscott who was the tenant of the King's Arms in Higher Market Street, which, under the grand plan, was to be demolished to make way for enlarged market facilities. Truscott did not, however, wish to have to take out two licences if the building works on the new inn went beyond September. In the event the new inn was not completed until 1822 and Truscott could breathe a sigh of relief.

It is possible that the delays in building of the new inn were exacerbated by the decay in the structure of the old Abbey House:

> "... they have nearly finished the roof which has been a troublesome thing owing to the decay of the timbers, although the front of the exterior is finished and they are now going on with the back part. The joiners and plaisterers are proceeding also with the interior as fast as they can make room for each other."

The period up to the opening of the hotel saw much correspondence between Bray, in Tavistock, and Adam, in the Bedford Estate Office in London, relating to the rental that Truscott was to be charged. Bray fought hard in Truscott's corner. Initially Truscott was to be given a tenancy for one year only and " ... if he conducted it well it would be as good as a lease of life for him ... it would operate as a stimulus to his exertions."

Bray must have felt that the Duke was to use the inn as a financial investment rather than as an act of benefaction for the people of Tavistock. If such was the case it could be readily seen that

Tavistock Vicarage pictured in 2009

The old Exeter Inn in the 1980s

the rental to be asked of Truscott was going to be unreasonable to his circumstances and prosperity. Bray wrote to Adam on 20 July 1821 stating –

> " ... you must not expect to make anything near the interest of the money laid out or the value of the premises according to the expense of building etc ... as no one could make it succeed in Tavistock."

After much debate between interested parties, Bray wrote to Adam on 21 November as follows

> "I have fully impressed on Truscott's mind the importance of attending to all the points you recommend and his views appear perfectly to agree with yours, and I have no doubt he will do all in his power to conduct the Inn in such a manner as to do him credit and give general satisfaction.
>
> On the subject of rent I would recommend you give him every encouragement for two or three years as the fitting up in that style of comfort and neatness, which he expresses his intention to do, will necessarily be a great expense, and which being a new thing will therefore be quite a risque and speculation – it must be considered also that the rates and taxes will amount to £70 a year exclusive of the excise licences etc, which I suppose will be £30 or more. I would therefore propose that he would occupy it rent free for the first year, or say until Ladyday 1823, the second year to pay £50 or £60, and afterwards £80 or £100 but I should not imagine he could ever afford more than that latter sum, altho' it will be far short of the interest of the money expended added to the value of the old premises."

Adam did not think too much of this proposition and accordingly Bray demonstrated diplomatic flexibility and obtained Adam's agreement as given in his letter to Bray of 6 December

> "I really think Truscott should pay a rent from the commencement and that of £50 cannot be considered at all unreasonable. I have no objection to let it increase £10 a year only till it reaches £100 and if we find the increase of business not to warrant such an advance then we can stop short. Do not however, enter into agreement of more than one year in writing. Let it be expressly stated that he is only to be tenant for a year notwithstanding the progressive increase of the rent. That only means that if he is retained whereupon the rent will be increased."

Whether Adam had no faith in Truscott's ability to run the top hotel in town is not stated in writing yet the insistence on a trial period of one year is consistently emphasised throughout the correspondence.

Whilst all the discussion on the rental was going on between the Stewards in Tavistock and London the building works were progressing. However, then, as now, building modification of this type brought its problems

> " ... There is one thing ... which appears to me to have been an oversight and ought to be remidied in some way or other, namely there is only one staircase in the plan

and unless a second flight is planned it will be very inconvenient as well as unpleasant to the visitors."

There were also minor aggravations with the new Plymouth Road being constructed at the same time

"We shall be obliged to take up and new make the road from the office down as far as the Vicarage House, as there was a mistake in the levels when it was first laid down and is two or three feet above the level of the turnpike opposite the old Bedford Arms."

Neither of the above 'faults' appear to have been remedied as far as can be ascertained. There is still only one staircase in the building which is shown at the opening of the hotel in 1822 ie the elegant, but small, staircase near the entrance to the present day restaurant; this staircase had three flights of which only two remain today, the lower flight having been removed at a time unknown. In addition the road level is still considerably higher than that at the Higher Abbey Gate. The troublesome level may have been lowered from the 'complaint' level but there remains a considerable crown visible in the road of today outside of the hotel entrance. That the road level sits part way up the ground floor windows enabled entrance through the main access door to the hotel.

Taperell's engraving of 1823 confirms the enlargement of the Abbey House to the new hotel, with the original 5 bayed, 3 storey, rectangular building on the left (east end); the cupola seen in the Delafontaine engraving of 1741 has been removed and the use of crenellations both on the old Abbey House and continuing into the new additions. Railings fronting the building protect a drop of some one metre down to the cobbled level of the early eighteenth century access to the building. The three storey building on the left of the new hotel is the Jacob Saunders Abbey House of 1725. The remaining structure(s) are thought to be mainly 1822 'new build' but it is known that some buildings were present at the west end of the Abbey House.

The cost of the conversion of the Abbey House was considerable being at least £6700, £280000 in today's money, and Bray did have his way in that many local tradesmen did benefit. Services and materials were supplied as follows

plumbing	John Abrahams, Fore Street; William Heard Lower Back Street
timber	Bayley (address not found)
plasterers	John Saunders, West Street; Francis Lovis, Brook Street
carpenters	William Martin, King Street
ironmongery	John Cornish, Market Place
carriage work	Archelaus Down, West Street
blacksmith	Jonathan Parford, West Street
paperwork	Miss Helms, Fore Street
iron work	John Gill, Ferrum Hill
lime, timber, brick	Gill and Co, Fore Street; Gilbert Northey, West Street
glaziers	John Martin, West Street
painters	Thomas Balch, West Street

Again, as is frequently the case, the cost of the alteration seems to have gone beyond budget or at least beyond expectations. It seems that William Bray was to be blamed for this mismanagement, a charge which he hotly denied. However, the mechanics of budgetary control and early settlement of accounts was somewhat slow as it was not until 29 August 1823 when Bray was to refute such accusations in a somewhat "not me guv' " style.

> "In reference to your heavy charge of mismanagement and unnecessary expence, I cannot conceive that it ought to apply to me, for I could not surely be held responsible for the correcting of the original estimate at the costly nature of the work done; the little that I have taken upon me to order was no more than was necessary for the convenience of the house or the security of the building – I don't need to inform you that estimates, in general, are far short of the actual expense of the buildings and particularly of old houses where it is hardly possible to calculate correctly what the expense of repairs or alterations will be."

Whether the deliberations over Truscott and the Bedford Hotel had blotted William Bray's copybook is not known but by 1823 Bray had reached the age of 70 and was replaced by the ascerbic Andrew Wilson as the Duke's Steward in Tavistock. Wilson does not appear to feature much in the future detail of the development of the Bedford Hotel from 1823 whereas the Brays had been instrumental in bringing about and completing the development.

No date has been found for the opening of the hotel but building works were likely completed in 1821. John Truscott paid rental from Ladyday 1822 and it is assumed that the Bedford Hotel opened shortly after that date. Certainly the Rentals Book for 1822/23 documented the conditions previously agreed between Bray and Adam as to Truscott's rental obligations

> "John Truscott, Bedford Arms Inn (late Abbey House), stables, yard and other offices, courtyard and garden behind the stables. At will, no heriots, no arrears; note to increase £10 per annum 'til amount is £100."

A further entry in the 1821/22 Rentals Book states that the Ball Room and rooms with garden attached, with lumber room under at the west end of the inn were 'in hand' and not rented to Truscott as part of the inn enterprise. On 19 August 1823 *The Times* newspaper had caught up with events and reported –

> "An excellent Inn has been lately built in the gothic style at Tavistock at the expense of the Duke of Bedford and it is to be in the contemplation of his Grace to restore in the same style, the exterior of the most interesting part of the remains of the Abbey."

Taperell's Directory of 1823 specifically notes the Bedford Hotel in the good hands of John Truscott with a Thomas Rowe as mine host in the hotel tap, which was under the main entrance to the hotel. The hotel seems to have been known for many years after its opening as the Bedford Arms Inn and is entered as such in the rentals books of the day up to at least 1841. The demolition of the Bedford Arms on the Higher Abbey Gate and the King's Arms in King Street were part of a grand plan to both enlarge the markets in Tavistock and to

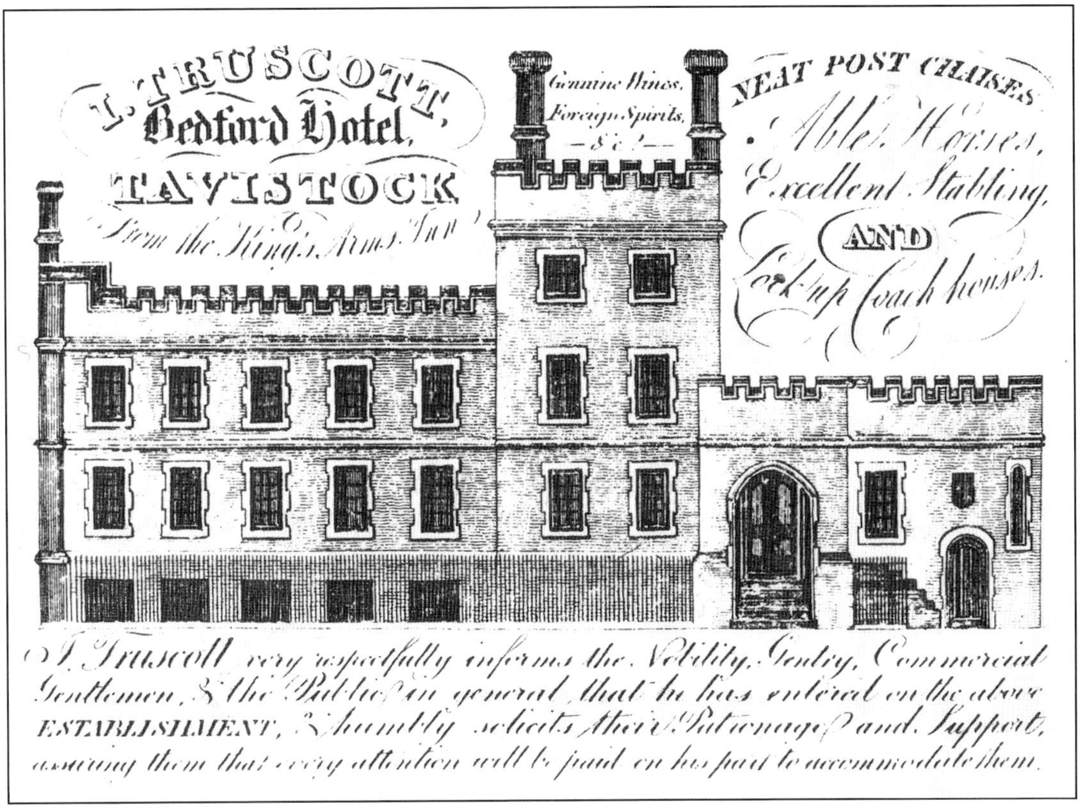

The Bedford Hotel after Taperell's Directory of 1823

Drain header with built date of 1821 and ducal coronet

Top flight of the original 1725 staircase in the Abbey House photographed in 2012 – note the original ceiling and cornice plasterwork at the stair head

undertake major works in that range of buildings now comprising Guildhall Square and Bank Square.

An engraving of the newly opened inn appears in Taperell's 1823 Directory for Plymouth and Tavistock, advertising the establishment thus

> "J Truscott very respectfully informs the Nobility, Gentry, Commercial Gentlemen and the Public in general that he has entered on the above establishment and humbly solicits their Patronage and Support assuring them that every attention will be paid on his part to accommodate them."

The hotel also advertised genuine wines, foreign spirits, neat post chaises, able horses, excellent stabling and lock-up coach houses. The directory also states that there was a regular coach service, The Independent Safety Coach, on Monday, Wednesday and Friday to and from Plymouth.

An interesting feature of the new hotel of 1823 is a ground level door in the building to the right hand of the entrance. This door is still extant in 2012 but although visible from outside how this

Painted by Sir Thos. Lawrence, P.R.A.

Engraved by H. Robinson.

SIR JEFFRY WYATVILLE. R.A. F.R.S_F.S.A.&c.

Sir Jeffry Wyatville (1766-1840) – copyright RIBA Library

door connected into what is now the Tavistock Room does not show internally. Similarly steps appear to go from the left hand side of this door to the level of the hotel reception area – reason not known today.

The modification of the Abbey House, into the Bedford Hotel, was admired by Britton and Brayley. They wrote of "the extensive imitative Gothic facade of the Bedford Arms Inn" which formed part of the commendable approach to the town (the New Plymouth Road). These authors attributed the design of the hotel to John Foulston, an architect responsible for many fine buildings in Plymouth and who did have working assignments in Tavistock in the early 1820s and later. Foulston was not, however, the architect responsible for the new Bedford Arms Inn. That task was assigned to Jeffry Wyatt (1766-1840), a man with many aristocratic patrons whose works included Endsleigh House, the Duke of Bedford's cottage in Milton Abbot, and the transformation of Windsor Castle in 1824, a commission which would have played a major role in his receiving a knighthood and becoming Sir Jeffry Wyatville in 1828.

At last John Truscott was to take up his new position and he must have done reasonably well as he held the tenancy until he died on 9 June 1834 at the early age of 53. On his death his estate went to his daughter Louisa, who had married Richard Gribbell, a Tavistock grocer, with £400 and an annual annuity of £10 to be paid out of the estate to his, John's, widow Elizabeth. Elizabeth died of 'natural decay', aged 73, in 1842 and she and John are buried in quiet solitude of Calstock churchyard. The memorial reads

> "To the memory of John Truscott of Tavistock Devon who died 29th June 1834 aged 53 years
> Also his grandson Henry Terrell Gribbell who died 6th April 1839 aged 2 years
> Also Elizabeth Truscott the wife of John Truscott who died 20th November 1842 aged 73 years
> Also Louisa E Pease daughter of the above and wife of Richd Gribbell who died 17th November 1855 …"

Louisa Elizabeth Pease Truscott was born c1809 in Lanteglos in Cornwall. She married Calstock born Richard Gribbell in April 1831 in Tavistock and they had at least 7 children all born in Tavistock, the youngest being John baptised in 1834.

Louisa Gribbell died in Tavistock 17 November 1855 aged 47 and Richard senior in Tavistock in 1861 age 62. The family had run a grocery business in Market Street for some 30 years up to Richard's death

It is possible that John Truscott, as well as his wife Elizabeth, was Cornish although the Truscott name does appear in earlier Tavistock parish church records. John's earliest appearance in printed records for Tavistock seems to be when he took over the King's Arms in Higher Market Street at Michaelmas 1820. The move for John Truscott and family to the Bedford was obviously an opportunity to run the premier hotel of the town and with the Duke's name to boot. However, the King's Arms was also a substantial well-established property paying rental of £52 10s in 1820.

The Truscott grave in Calstock churchyard

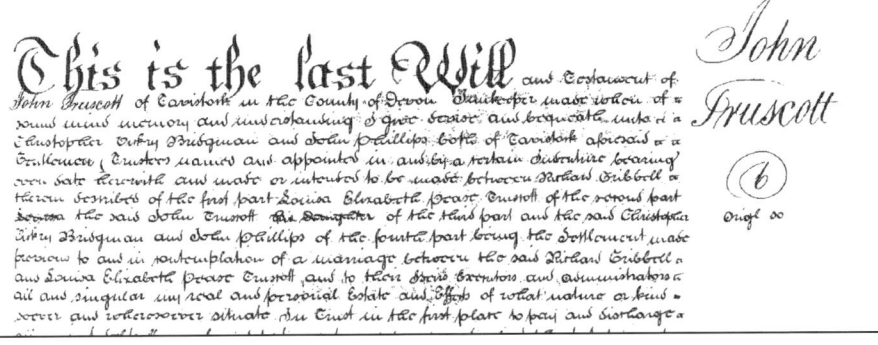

The opening passages of John Truscott's Last Will and Testament dated 29 April 1836

The Will reads

"This is the last Will and Testament of John Truscott of Tavistock in the County of Devon Innkeeper made when of sound mind memory and understanding I give devise and bequeath unto Christopher Vickry Bridgman and John Phillips both of Tavistock aforesaid Gentlemen trustees named and appointed in and by a certain Indenture bearing even date herewith and made or intended to be made between Richard Gribbell therein described of the first part Louisa Elizabeth Pease Truscott of the second part the said John Truscott of the third part and the said Christopher Vickry Bridgman and John Phillips of the fourth part being the Settlement made provision to and in contemplation of a marriage between the said Richard Gribbell and Louisa Elizabeth Pease Truscott and to their heirs executors and administrators all and singular my real and personal estate and effects of what nature or kind soever and wheresoever situate In Trust in the first place to pay and discharge ..."

The conversion of the Abbey House into the Bedford Hotel needs to be seen as part of a grand strategy for Tavistock to consolidate the non-livestock markets mainly in the Market Street/King Street area of the town, to 'tidy up' parts of the Abbey site and make further investment in the ducal estate to optimise financial return. Within a year of the new Bedford Hotel being opened the old Bedford Arms was demolished, clearing the way for further development in this area. In the same year the King's Arms was also demolished, opening up what is now Bank Square for use as a market place. These were but first moves in the grand plan and over the next ten to twenty years more investment was to follow. Unfortunately the documentation within the surviving Bedford Papers most often collects expenditure vouchers together for a number of projects and it is nigh impossible to derive the costs of many of the individual projects.

In addition to the above other works were undertaken including

> – As early as 1823 work was undertaken to maintain the fabric of the ballroom of the Abbey House, the ballroom not being rented to Truscott.

> – In 1823/24 the western wall of the churchyard opposite the hotel was demolished and rebuilt "to form a footpath to the Inn" from West Street passing Church Bow. This footpath is in full use today.

> – Improvements such as a new hotel sign, lamps, bells were undertaken in 1825/6.

> – In 1826/7 new parlours were added within the hotel plus 'two new rooms'.

Then came the bigger projects.

> – In 1827 through 1831 a stable block was built from the ballroom on the east to the old Abbey boundary to the west and then north along this wall. This addition to the hotel can be seen on the enlarged 1831 Ordnance Survey Map of Tavistock, despite the small size of this map.

> – In 1830 through 1832 many expenditures can be seen in the Bedford Estate Papers, especially in the Rentals Books, detailing the works on the new ballroom and the lumber room beneath.

> – Alongside these works other big projects were undertaken including the building of the new Subscription Library east of Higher Abbey Gate and the Bedford Estate Office immediately east of the hotel

One thing is clear from the disbursements recorded in the Bedford archive and that is that the tradesmen were again, as with the transformation of Abbey House, locally based and many of the names given in the 1820s carried on providing professional services for the alterations. However, the elegant new ballroom was the work of the eminent Plymouth architect John Foulston (1772-1842) who also undertook works for the Bedford Estate in Guildhall Square. Foulston was a pupil of Thomas Hardwick and set up practice in London in 1796. In 1810 he won a competition to design the Royal Hotel, Athenaeum and Assembly Rooms and many other

John Foulston (1772-1842) – copyright RIBA Library

prominent buildings in Plymouth where he eventually resided and worked as a leading architect for some 25 years. The money, contacts and influence of the house of Bedford was a continuing draw for this renowned architect who was to undertake further works in Tavistock after the completion of the ballroom.

The new ballroom replaced the old Gothic room described by Mrs Bray, a well-known Victorian authoress and wife of Edward Atkyns Bray, vicar of Tavistock from 1812 to 1857. In one of her letters to Robert Southey Mrs Bray said of the old ball room

> "I have omitted to mention that the old ball-room, erroneously called the Refectory, stood nearly north by south: it is on the first floor: and I have reason to think communicated with what was considered the Abbot's Hall ... by means of a gallery. The old ballroom had also a passage of communication with the Abbey House. Whilst my father lived there, several years since, I restored some of the windows, which had been plastered over when the mullions of the others were destroyed for the purpose of introducing modern sash windows; the taste, I conclude, of Mr Saunders who seems to have spared neither labour nor expense to do all the mischief he could possibly effect. The windows thus restored had a beautiful appearance. The ceiling was modern, being somewhat vaulted, but broken in the curve by a moulding, and then becoming flat. As it was much decayed it was taken down, when the original roof became visible, but so little of it remained that I dared not recommend the restoration, but contented myself with giving it an uninterrupted curve. The wood-work, as well as I recollect, was of a trefoil form, elegantly but not very richly carved."

In her paper on Tavistock Abbey in 1929 Lady Radford touches upon the old ballroom referred to by Mrs Bray and suggests that this old ballroom was developed from the great kitchen of the Abbey. In a lease of 1691 this building had vaults and cellars beneath it, the ballroom being on the first floor.

Foulston's new ballroom was considered "very handsome" and there would appear to be no accusations against either Foulston or his employer, the Duke of Bedford, of partaking of villainous acts by destroying yet another part of the original Abbey buildings. In 1833 Mrs Bray describes her experiences of the new building

> "The old Gothic Room ... was, about three years ago, taken down, and a very handsome ball-room erected in its stead by the duke. I have been in it but twice: the first time was on a ball night, when from its size and the comparatively small company assembled, it was dreadfully cold, and I sat shivering all the evening, wishing for the old room; the dancers, however, did not complain. Since then we have had one concert in it, in which there was one good vocal performer, Miss Elizabeth Greco, who sings indeed delightfully ... From hearing our Miss Greco, I found the new room was admirably adapted for music ... "

Access to the ballroom was via two doors leading from a reception area at the north end.

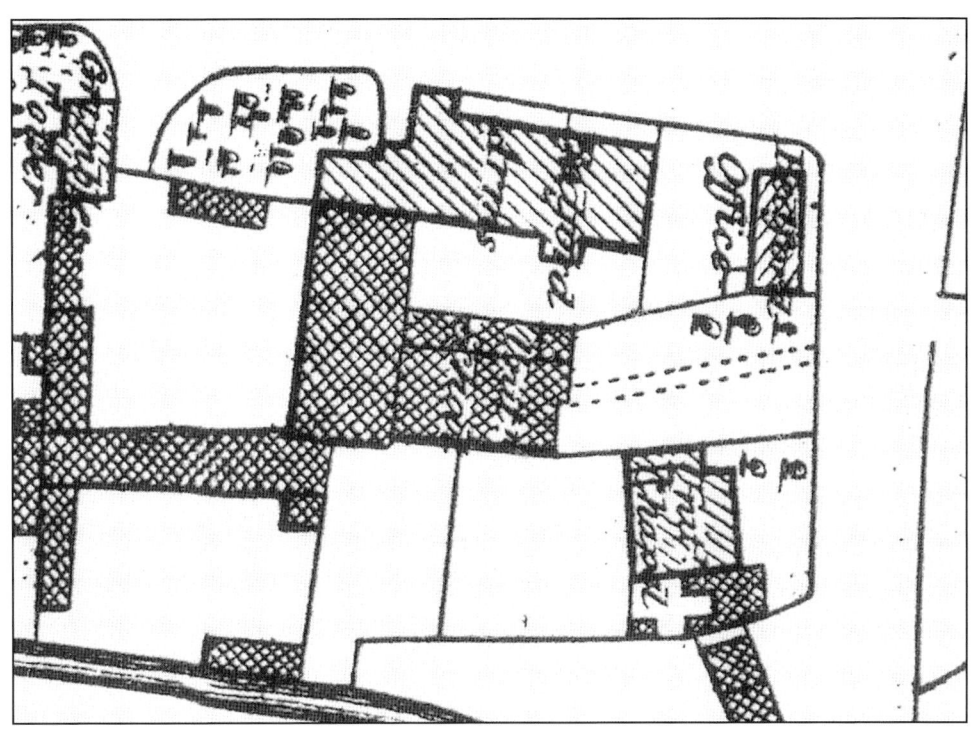

A ground plan of the Bedford Hotel site from the 1842 Tavistock Town Map. The map section shows the ballroom running at right angles to the Bedford Hotel and adjoins with what is erroneously described as the Unitarian School but is, in fact, the Unitarian Chapel. The new stable block attaches to the end of the ballroom.

The new ballroom of 1830 after John Foulston. Access to the ballroom was via two doors from a reception area shown at the far end

Detail of ballroom ceiling plasterwork c1830 – extant 2012

Plaster cornice work at the entrance area to the 1830's ballroom likely fabricated at that time – extant 2012

From the engraving of the Bedford Hotel on its opening in 1822 it is seen that the west end clearly comprised an extension to the Abbey House, the extension housing a four storey castellated tower plus the main entrance and other room(s) at entrance level with rooms under. The earliest photograph found of the west end clearly shows another storey having been built above the main entrance and to the west, and then south, with the castellated roof being contiguous with and north of the 1830's ballroom. The whole of the western elevation of the ballroom is rendered as with the contiguous two-storey face. The new storey above the entrance going west connects at like height with the roofline of the 1830s ballroom and its northern addition. However, the non-rendered north western corner at first floor level clearly shows a building of rubble stone as opposed to Hurdwick stone used for the main hotel; in addition the roof line is contiguous with that of the new ballroom.

The Truscott advertisement of 1823 clearly states 'excellent stabling and lock-up coach houses' and whether the new stable block replaced earlier provisions, or whether stabling was provided elsewhere within Tavistock, is not known.

Even as late as 1834 the ballroom and other parts of the site are not rented to Truscott, which does seem strange; perhaps trust in Truscott's ability had, still, not yet been established.

On the 25th of March 1835 (Ladyday) another Cornishman was to become lessee of the hotel; Mr John Taunton took over from the executors of John Truscott, at an increased rental of £122 a year. In celebration of his new tenancy Taunton arranged a dinner for some of the local gentry. The occasion rated a report in *The Exeter Flying Post* of 5 March

> "A party of 70 gentlemen dined together on Thursday last at the Bedford Hotel, Tavistock, to celebrate the succession of Mr Taunton to that establishment. John Carpenter, of Mount Tavy, presided, supported by J Janes Esq, and other gentlemen of the town and neighbourhood. The dinner as well as the manner of serving it up did great credit to the new landlord and the wines were of the choicest descriptions."

The census return of 1841 gives the first opportunity to look at both the live-in manning levels and the guests present on census night of 7 June 1841. Neither mine host John Taunton, age 46, nor his wife Mary, age 43, were born in Devon, neither were their first two daughters aged 23 and 19; their two younger daughters, aged 17 and 16 were. Two servants and eight guests made up the house complement on that night.

By 1843 John Taunton had given up his residency of the Bedford and at 30 March 1851 is found, age 53, a horse trainer, with Mary, his wife, age 52, and a daughter Elizabeth, 28, all born in Liskeard, living in Wroughton in Wiltshire. By 1861 John, now given as a retired farmer, and Mary, were living in St Pancras with their unmarried daughter Elizabeth. Mary died in St Pancras in 1873 and John in Thanet Registration District in 1883 aged 86.

Taunton's successor was Edmund Lakeman Elliott. He had taken up residence with his wife Elizabeth and their first three children, daughters Bessie, Kate and Emma, who were born in the Bedford Hotel in 1843, 1845 and 1846 respectively and baptised in St Eustachius's Church,

Tavistock. In 1843 Edmund was aged 23 and his wife Elizabeth, 26, relatively young to be running such a prestigious establishment. The Elliott family were Devon born, Edmund was a native of Ugborough and Elizabeth of Devonport; they had married by licence in Stoke Damerel parish church on the 19th of September 1842 and a year later they were in place in the Bedford for the birth of Bessie who was baptised in St Eustachius's Church on 30 September 1843.

The art of innkeeping should have been well known to Edmund and his wife as they both came from innkeeping stock. Edmund Elliott's father was an innkeeper in charge of the Royal Hotel in Fore Street, Devonport, with his wife Mary, in the early 1830s and 1840s. The Royal was large and at 1841 census the household comprised William senior and his wife Mary, three children, fourteen servants and thirteen others (likely guests at the inn) ie a house comparable in size to the Bedford. Next door on the north side of Fore Street lived another innkeeping family headed by John and Jane Townshend with their three children, including Edmund's future wife Elizabeth, aged 24. The Townshends ran the London Inn, Devonport.

Edmund Elliott appears to have had an affinity for coach travel as during his period of tenancy at the Bedford Hotel there seems to have been an increase of coach traffic running to and from the hotel. This is, perhaps, not surprising as coach building was a skill well known to him, his father William and his elder brother Thomas were both given as coachbuilders when the family lived in Devonport., and they were running a coachbuilders' business at the Tamar Coach Factory in Morice Town in 1844. At the Royal Inn, advertised in Devonport in 1830, coach travel featured prominently. In Tavistock in 1844 Edmund offered the following coach services from the Bedford Hotel

> "The Telegraph to Barnstaple on Tuesdays, Thursdays and Saturdays; the Nicholas Omnibus to Callington on Wednesdays and to Okehampton on Saturdays; The Royal Mail to Exeter every evening and to Plymouth every morning; Nicol's and Down's Omnibus to Plymouth on Monday, Tuesday, Thursday and Saturday; Scott's and Cobbledick's Omnibus on Wednesday."

It was not just Elliott's presence that secured coaching services for the Bedford for as early as 1823 a coach ran from the hotel to Plymouth and Dock three times a week at four in the afternoon. There was no commercial traffic advertised in the local directories from the hotel in 1830 and by 1838 only Royal Mail coaches to Launceston and Devonport are so advertised. During Elliott's time in the Bedford the commercial traffic to and from the hotel increased markedly and after he had moved on c1850 such services appear to have ceased. By 1852 the only advertised coach or omnibus service to/from the hotel was the Royal Mail to Launceston every morning at half past eight and every evening at seven; and to Plymouth and Devonport every morning at eight and every afternoon at four. By 1856 the only Royal Mail coach running from Tavistock was from the Exeter Inn at eight in the morning, nothing at all to or from the Bedford. Tavistock's first railway opened in June 1859 having already reached Plymouth in 1848 and this railway link put paid to the Royal Mail and other coach services via the Bedford. However, the hotel was listed as a Posting House in the commercial directories until 1902. Commercial coaches, omnibuses and carriers ran from the other inns in Tavistock but after 1856 the only commercial traffic of this kind were the omnibuses to meet the trains.

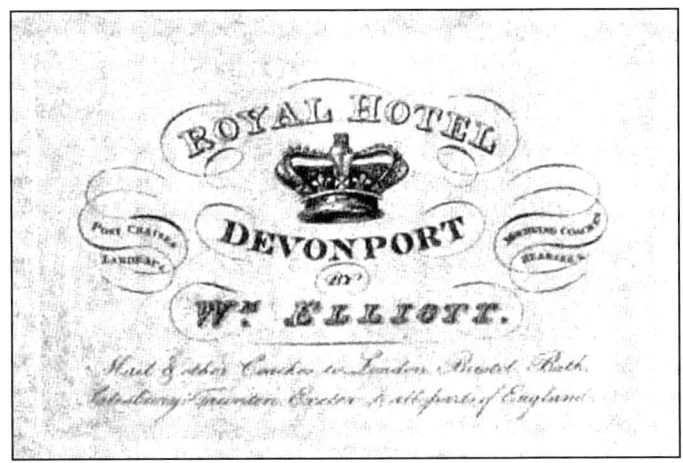

Advert for William Elliott's Royal Hotel from Brindley's Plymouth Directory for 1830 offering "Mail & other Coaches to London, Bristol, Bath, Salisbury, Taunton, Exeter & all parts of England."

Advert for Townshend's London Inn in Devonport, from Brindley's Plymouth Directory of 1830. The inn also boasts weekly coach travel to Bath, Bristol and London, through Dorchester, Blandford and Salisbury and a daily coach to London " ... over the new line of Road, in 26 hours".

NAVAL AND COMMERCIAL HOUSE.

Townshend's London Inn,

FORE-STREET, DEVONPORT.

The above House has been recently fitted up in a superior manner, for the reception of

Families, Commercial Gentlemen,

and the Public generally,

with GOOD BEDS, STABLING, and every other accommodation.

THE

CELERITY COACH,

Every Morning, at EIGHT o'Clock, to Bath, Bristol, and London, through Dorchester, Blandford, and Salisbury.

THE

SUBSCRIPTION COACH,

Every Day, at TWELVE o'Clock, to LONDON, OVER THE NEW LINE OF ROAD, IN 26 HOURS!

The Bedford Hotel throughout its history was to be the venue for many local events of importance and, sometimes, beneficence. In Elliott's tenancy, in January 1847, a public meeting was called by the Tavistock portreeve, Henry Terrell, to discuss, and, hopefully, pledge funds for, the relief of those badly affected by the potato crop failure due to potato blight in Ireland and Scotland. Some 28 persons attended, all members of the local elite, and doubtless amid much enjoyment of fine food, ale and wine certain pledges were made; whether such pledges included monetary contributions by the individual attendees is not recorded but there was a commitment to launch a local campaign to provide food, funds and clothing for the starving of Ireland and Scotland – this could mean the rich and the good expected others to pay rather than themselves but such thoughts of mischief are, indeed, very unkind.

The Elliott tenancy was relatively short as by April 1851 the family were living in Tamar Green in Stoke Damerel where Edmund was back to his true love as a coachbuilder employing 44 men. The family subsequently moved on to Landulph and by 1861 Edmund was given in the census return as a retired coachmaker. His wealth did not protect his health; Edmund died in St Germans District in 1869 at the early age of 49, Elizabeth surviving him by only some 7 years.

Whether Edmund's leaving the Bedford had anything to do with a hankering for coachbuilding is not known but Edmund's generation of the Elliott dynasty were seemingly not long lived, his brother Thomas Elliott, also a coachbuilder, of Tamar Wharf, Devonport died in his thirties in June of 1850 and Thomas's will is intriguing as he instructs that his coachbuilding business is to be sold by his Trustees who are named as William Edwin Elliott, his brother, John Widdicombe, his brother-in-law, and William Lavers the younger. Within two months of Thomas's death adminstration of the Will, on 17 August 1850, was passed to Edmund Lakeman Elliott, another of Thomas's brother. By some eight months later Edmund Lakeman Elliott, aged 31, was the owner of the coachbuilding business.

A point of interest was the other Elliott brother named in Thomas's will, namely William Edwin Elliott, who was, in 1850, running the Royal Hotel in Plymouth, a most prestigious establishment after John Foulston c1812 and immediately adjacent to the famous Athenaeum of the same date. In 1867 William Edwin Elliott died in Plympton and by 1871 a Samuel Pearse is given as running the Royal Hotel. At the end of the century a Pearse family descendant and the Royal Hotel were linked with the Bedford Hotel – such coincidences are the stuff of speculation and intrigue by family historians and, maybe, we should 'watch this space'.

Whether or not Edmund Lakeman Elliott was an unsuitable tenant as far as the Bedford Estate was concerned or whether Edmund just wished to move back to coachbuilding is not known but in August 1848 Benson, the Duke's steward in Tavistock, wrote to Hardy, the chief steward in London, stating that he, Benson, was advertising the Bedford and that he had someone interested in taking over. In the event two offers for the tenancy seem to have been the front runners viz one from a Mr Killingley for £170 a year and one from a Mr Northway for £150 a year. For Benson Killingley was the preferred new tenant but when the time came for the change over of tenants Killingley and Elliott fell out as described in Benson's correspondence

"Killingley not agreeing to take Elliott's furniture entire ... Elliott will not leave,

48

❖THE "ROYAL,"❖
PLYMOUTH.

First-Class Family Hotel.

LADIES' DRAWING ROOM.

SPACIOUS GENERAL COFFEE ROOM.

SMOKING AND WRITING ROOM.

SUPERIOR STABLING.

Every variety of Carriage for Posting and Excursions.

Omnibuses attend every train, Great Western and South Western.
Carriages if ordered.

S. PEARSE ~ ~ ~ ~ Proprietor.

Advertisement for Samuel Pearse's Royal Hotel Plymouth in 1879

so that all the trouble taken is so much lost labour ... Elliott will injure the house the longer he holds it with the knowledge that he is to go."

Finally the new tenant for the Bedford was agreed and William Rowe Northway moved from Tavistock's second inn, the Exeter Inn, in 1849. Northway offered £170 per annum, acceptable to Benson and Co, but doing nothing to prevent acrimony again between the outgoing Elliott and the now prospective tenant, Northway.

During the period of change of tenants in the hotel it was likely 'business as usual'. On the 4th of August 1848 the *Plymouth, Devonport and Stonehouse Herald* announced that the first exhibition of the newly formed Tavistock Cottage Garden Society was to take place in the ballroom of the Bedford Hotel on the 24th of that month. The paper duly gave a report of the event

" ... the ballroom ... was tastefully decorated for the occasion. The ladies and gentlemen of the town and neignbourhood assisted very materially by depositing the beauties of their greenhouses to enrich the collection, and everything was done by the committee to render the show attractive. The exhibition was a very excellent one, the fruits, flowers, and vegetables being particularly worthy of notice ... The company was numerous and respectable, a band was in attendance, the church bells rang merry peals, and everything wore the appearance of a holiday…"

The Tavistock Cottage Garden Society was to hold their annual exhibition in the Bedford for the next two years after which it moved to the Cornmarket and eventually to the Pannier Market building and in 1849 the "the display of fruits, flowers, plants and vegetables was far superior to that of last year". From the press reports during those three years the event at the Bedford appears to have been likely more for the 'posh' to see the efforts of 'the others'. In 1849 the event was again reported in the *Plymouth, Devonport and Stonehouse Herald* viz

"The day being very fine, a numerous and highly respectable company were present, amongst whom were many of the first families of the neighbourhood ... After the prizes were awarded, about seventy gentlemen sat down to a sumptuous dinner ..."

Likely not many 'cottagers' were present at the dinner although it would certainly have been these persons who provided the core of the 50 exhibits. However, the cottagers could rest assured that the great and the good did have their interests at heart and after the 1850 exhibition and dinner John Rundle, President of the Society and local dignatory, said in his speech

"I would like to see every labouring man have two suits of working clothes, as I am convinced that nothing would more tend to the health and comfort of these poor men than having a change of raiment instead of wearing wet clothes, as was too often the case, day by day."

The exact date of Elliott's departure from the hotel is difficult to determine but Elliott was 'under notice' in 1848 and Northway was 'in house' in 1850; a date of 1849 for the transfer fits well with contemporary evidence.

The Northway family had been tenants of the Exeter Inn in King Street since at least 1793 and William Northway (1760-1832) was to be the tenant there until his death 'in situ'. He was born in Chagford in 1760 and had married Ann Boyer in Chagford in 1789. Their first-born child, John, was to move to Tavistock with the family c1792 where a further five little Northways were born, likely in the Exeter Inn in Back Street, which William took over in 1793 and ran until his death in September 1832. Ann had died in 1802 and, six months after Ann's death, William married Susanna Rowe in Chagford. On 22 November 1808 William Rowe Northway was baptised in St Eustachius's Church, Tavistock, undoubtedly to much liquid rejoicing later that day, which would have been an appropriate start in life for William junior was to take over the Exeter Inn on the death of his father and be mine host in that important inn until the greater prize of the Bedford Hotel became available in 1850. The Northway family had thus completed 57 years as tenants of the Exeter Inn; William's half-brother John and his family were to see out 85 years in the Queen's Head in West Street and now William Rowe Northway was to start a career in the Bedford for the next 37 years – a magnificent family effort to the cause of drink of some 179 man years.

William Rowe Northway and his wife Sally (nee Ryall) had two surviving children when they moved to the Bedford viz Mary Rowe born 1837 and William Rowe junior born 1844. Sally was from the neighbouring parish of Milton Abbot and had married William in the parish church there on 6 April 1836.

During the Northway tenancy of the Bedford the hotel was described as a "family and commercial hotel and posting house" and Northway himself variously as a victualler; innkeeper; wine, spirit, ale and porter merchant and farmer. The hotel provided public entertainments in the Assembly Rooms (the Ball Room) and many events of great local significance were to affect the hotel and it would appear that Northway had quickly established a reputation for the hotel; Samuel Rowe, in his work entitled A Perambulation of the Ancient and Royal Forest of Dartmoor published in 1855, wrote

> " … we shall close our excursion at the Bedford Hotel, and the traveller must be fastidious indeed; who would complain of the accommodation he will find at one of the best inns, in one of the most interesting towns, in the west of England."

The local press recorded a New Year Ball in November 1857 and that the Tavistock elite were dancing until four o'clock in the morning. Many dances, meetings and events of local importance chose the Assembly Rooms as the preferred venue, including local political candidates preaching their views to their potential followers. In one case the hotel even acted as a haven of refuge from the sticks and stones of the dissenting electorate. In April 1852 the candidates gave election addresses in the Assembly Rooms and in 1858, following the resignation of the local MP Mr Byng, Arthur Russell, nephew of the then Duke of Bedford, and Edward Miall met in the Assembly Rooms where the nomination took place. At the polling next day Arthur Russell won the day. At the General Election in April 1859 Northway provided 'committee room' facilities for the candidates.

The hotel was recognised in its own right as a recommended place for the great and the good to stay and meet as confirmed by Anthony Trollope (1815-1882), one of the most prolific and successful novelists of the Victorian era. Trollope's novels were, in some cases at least, clearly based on his own life experiences and such included staying at the Bedford Hotel, as part of his travels in Devon when he worked for the Post Office. In his book The Three Clerks (1858) Trollope writes about two travellers from London taking the train to Plymouth and then chaise to Tavistock for the purpose of inspecting a mine for possible investment. The mine, unnamed, was potentially the most prolific mine in the country at the time and was likely part of the Devon Great Consols mining group.

After their long journey and upon arriving late at night at the Bedford the travellers partook of tea

> "They were soon drinking tea together at the Bedford Hotel and I beg to assure any travelling readers that they might have drunk tea in a much worse place."

The coming of the railway to Tavistock was celebrated in 1859 with the broad gauge Brunel built line of the South Devon Railway (later to be taken over by GWR in 1878). The railway opened on 21 June 1859 and the railway directors were entertained at the Bedford at a 'dejeuner' hosted by the portreeve, Mr C H Daw, where some 120 guests sat down "to a most excellent dinner provided by Mr Northway … whose admirable catering left nothing to be desired." The whole town was decorated "… which imparted to the town a gay and animated appearance" and the Bedford Hotel made its contribution

> "… The portico of the Bedford Hotel was ornamented with evergreens and flowers, while an arch of immense, but well preserved proportions, spanned the street. In addition to numerous flags, it bore the mottoes, "success to the iron road," "time is money," "prosperity to commerce", and "increase to trade."

As well as a huge procession through the town comprising of the great, the good, the workers and those wishing to advertise their wares the *Tavistock Gazette* noted that subscriptions had been raised to provide a public tea in the streets for four thousand people, followed by music, dancing and fireworks. True to form "… just about tea time, the rain began to descend, though happily not so as seriously to inconvenience the tea drinkers."

Despite the ballroom being put into good use as assembly rooms etc for Tavistock there was a growing swell of local opinion that Tavistock deserved better facilities for public meetings. Under a lead article entitled "One of the great social wants of the town" the *Tavistock Gazette* of 13 November 1857 began, with its usual flowery prose, to arouse interest in securing such facilities.

> "… Each type of civilisation and progress takes its chief impression from our social organisation. If this is defective, our institutions for mental and moral improvement will be stunted and weakened. Every advantage should be given to the improved social mechanism of the age. The wants of the people should be satisfied and their reasonable claims should be met. Our town does not afford adequate means to meet them. We have no assembly room equal to the wants of the age and place. The result is, that when a great social treat is provided, incurring a considerable expenditure, the price of admission is necessarily high – too high for families of moderate resources

Advertisements for events in the Ballroom (Assembly Rooms) of the Bedford Hotel in 1857

to reach. The excluded are annoyed, blame is thrown upon the managers and the elements of discord disturb the whole community. A larger room which would give accommodation to at least 700 or 800 people would correct the evil. Could not this be supplied in the intended new building for the market? ..."

These early years of Northway's tenancy of the hotel were exciting days indeed for Tavistock, not only for the coming of the railway and high social events but a huge town centre redevelopment orchestrated and paid for by the House of Bedford and enabled by the Tavistock Market Act of 1859. A large part of the south-eastern part of the town was demolished and in its place arose a New Town Hall, a new Market and also Duke Street, a splendid street of fine Victorian buildings housing retail premises. Thus the plea for a larger venue for public events was heard and the 'evil' corrected and many larger public events were held in the Pannier Market hall which opened in 1862 and in the new Town Hall opened in 1863. The Bedford Hotel Assembly Rooms still continued in use for many more years, generally catering for the more literate and/or the wealthy. For example the railway directors must have liked the hotel reception for the opening of the railway in 1859 as they returned there for another binge in 1876 when the broad gauge rail change to standard gauge had been completed. That day, also, offered one of those opportunities for Victorian Tavistock to demonstrate what it could do in terms of public rejoicing for a notable event, the town being gloriously decorated. Mr Northway and the Bedford Hotel joined in the celebrations with the entrance portico being decorated in " ... a perfect hothouse aspect, considerable taste being displayed in the arrangement of the flowers ... ", the hotel display having a similar ring to the display for the opening of the railway in 1859.

The railway opened up the town of Tavistock for tourism and trade even though it was to lead to the slow, very slow, demise of the horse drawn coach, omnibus and carrier traffic as well as the closure for trade of the Tavistock Canal. The railway was a good opportunity for the Bedford Hotel and guest numbers would have increased although no documented evidence supporting this survives apart from sparse real time spots from the census returns, which may well be non-representative due to persons wishing to record from their home base for the census. To ensure guaranteed best service for rail travellers the Bedford omnibus met visitors at the station and returned them so as to alight their trains on departure – all part of the service, sir.

(NB – In 1896 a waggonette omnibus was built by Budge and Co of Lumburn, just outside of Tavistock for John Backwell of the Cornish Arms in West Street this waggonette was used, among other duties, for the station service for the Bedford Hotel. This carriage was taken out of service with special ceremonies in 1930 but the omnibus itself still exists in working order today, having undergone sympathetic restoration by the current owner, Mr Gerald Williamson of Tavistock.)

Some events celebrated at the hotel were of enormous local importance. In the *Plymouth, Devonport and Stonehouse Herald* of 26 July 1856 is described the opening of the British and Foreign School in Plymouth Road on 19 July, an occasion which was attended not only by the Duke and Duchess of Bedford but also by the Duke's brother, Lord John Russell, Prime Minister from 1846 to 1852, and later to be so again from 1865 to 1866. This was an occasion of 'must attend' for Tavistock society and later, after the Duke and Lord John had driven to Endsleigh (perhaps for alcoholic 'tea' and men's talk), there was an opportunity to mingle with

ANNO VICESIMO SECUNDO

VICTORIÆ REGINÆ.

****

Cap. xxxiii.

An Act for constructing Market Houses and other
Buildings, and making Market Places, and for
better regulating and maintaining the Markets
and Fairs in or near the Town of *Tavistock;*
and for opening a new Street, and otherwise
improving the said Town ; and for other Pur-
poses.   [19th *April* 1859.]

WHEREAS Markets and Fairs have been for many Years
held in or near the Town of *Tavistock* in the County of
Devon, for the Sale of Live Cattle and other Live Stock, Corn,
Meat, Poultry, Eggs, Butter, Fish, Fruit, Vegetables, Hay, Straw, and
Merchandise, Manufactures, and other marketable Commodities : And
whereas the said Markets have been held partly in the Butchers and Corn
and Butter and Poultry Markets, but chiefly in the public Streets and
open Places of the Town, to the great Inconvenience and Danger of the
Inhabitants thereof, and of Persons resorting thereto : And whereas the
Most Noble *Francis* Duke of *Bedford,* Knight of the Most Noble Order
of the Garter, is or claims to be seised in Fee or absolutely entitled to the
Manors of *Tavistock* and *Hurdwick* in the County of *Devon,* and is in like

The front page of the Tavistock Markets Act of 1859

The Budge and Co 1896 waggonette used by Backwell for the Bedford Hotel station service – photo 2010

the elite offered by an all-ticket real 'tea' at the Bedford. The description of the event is a wonderful example of journalism in Victorian England and also how one went about such occasions.

"At six o'clock a large party sat down to tea in the ball-room of the Bedford Hotel. The Duchess of Bedford sat at the head of the centre table. The room was beautifully decorated and had a very brilliant appearance; and the cheerful cup and its concomitants appeared to have been greatly enjoyed by the ladies and gentlemen present. The admission was by ticket; and many persons who had not availed themselves of an early opportunity for procuring them, were greatly disappointed at being deprived of the honour of taking tea with her Grace. The Duchess, who was elegantly dressed in white silk – a white silk scarf, trimmed with scarlet; white silk bonnet with elegant flowers – looked in excellent health and spirits, and appeared highly to enjoy the scene, both in the school-room and at the tea table.

The tables were replenished for those who had not been in time for the first party.

At the conclusion, Mr Gill, who had so ably presided at the public meeting, proposed a vote of thanks to the ladies, and particularly to the Duchess of Bedford, for having honoured the opening ceremony with their presence, and also for their kindness in presiding at the tea-tables.

The Rev Mr Paul had great pleasure in seconding the resolution. He felt assured that everyone present would manifest their interest in the schools which had been opened that day, by endeavouring, as far as was in their power, to promote the spread of popular education. It afforded him great gratification to tender to the Duchess of Bedford his best thanks for her support on that and every other occasion, and for the earnest desire her Grace had at all times, evinced to promote the welfare of the inhabitants of Tavistock and neighbourhood.

These observations were received with great applause; and the resolution was carried by acclamation. Thus concluded the interesting ceremony of the day."

Little fingers crooked everybody!

The coming of age party of John Carpenter of Mount Tavy in February of 1860 was celebrated when the "tenantry took part in a dinner at the Bedford Hotel." At the same time schoolchildren were treated to teas in the Corn Market and the inmates of the Workhouse were given a substantial meal at Mount Tavy. As we can see the provision of 'tea' was not confined to entertaining the children as part of public events.

In 1864 perhaps the richest guest ever, Baroness Angela Burdett Coutts, the wealthy Victorian philanthropist, visited the hotel during a visit to see her friend Sir James Brooke, the first Rajah of Sarawak, who lived at Sheepstor. Sir James Brooke and the baroness enjoyed a decade of correspondence over the period 1858 until Sir James's death in 1868. Baroness Coutts had inherited three million pounds from her grandfather in 1837, worth some two to three hundred million pounds today. It is to be hoped that she gave generously to the Band of the 22nd Volunteer Regiment that played a selection of music outside the hotel in her honour.

It was custom and practice at election time in Tavistock that the prospective candidates stayed overnight in the Bedford, a practice already seen in the Bedford Arms in 1768 when Rigby was returned unopposed. Sometimes the going did, however, get a little energetic for a quiet country town hotel. At the General Election of 1865 the local favourite, Samuel Carter, was soundly beaten by a London man, Mr Samuda. The situation is described by local historian Gerry Woodcock (in press)

> "The crowd that assembled at the hustings to hear the declaration of the result consisted mainly of supporters of Samuel Carter, some of them enfranchised, many not. They were angry. The stranger from London, the man who represented the big industrial and financial interests, had defeated the local boy, the people's champion. The atmosphere of noise and disorder became so threatening that Samuda, having made a number of attempts to begin a victory speech, gave up, stepped down from the hustings, and began to walk the fifty yards to the Bedford Hotel where he was staying. He was surrounded by a group and jostled. Some in the mob brandished sticks and staves, and some stones were thrown. Within seconds other missiles were flying through the air …"

The Duke of Bedford also used his principal inn to entertain his tenants and freeholders of the town. Family celebrations were a good excuse for a fling and the Duke paid for a good party in the town in October 1876 when his eldest son got married at the family seat in Woburn. The local paper gave the event good coverage

"Tavistock has this week surrendered itself to a round of festivities, hospitably and munificently provided by His Grace the Duke of Bedford, in celebration of the marriage of his elder son, the Marquis of Tavistock. On Tuesday the ringing of the bells and the firing of cannon announced that the happy event had taken place, while numerous flags, and the crowds of well-dressed people in the streets, gave to the town the appearance of a general holiday. At three o'clock the tenantry and others, to the number of nearly five hundred, assembled in the market, to partake of a splendid banquet, and in the evening a display of fireworks gratified some thousands of spectators. A ball in the town hall, very numerously attended, concluded the day. On Wednesday the schoolchildren of the town and immediate neighbourhood, to the number of twelve or thirteen hundred, paraded the streets with music and banners, and were afterwards regaled with an abundant tea. On Thursday the workman of the estates were provided with dinner at the Town Hall, while today the old people will share in the general rejoicings, and next week the inmates of the Workhouse will be the guests of the Duke. Similar rejoicings have been held in Bedfordshire. Thus widely and heartily has a joyful family event been celebrated, and if the Marquis and his bride realise all the happiness that has been wished for them, their course through life will be one of perpetual sunshine."

The dinner in the Pannier Market, for five hundred people, was provided by William Northway of the Bedford Hotel. The menu indicates the fare that the inn would provide in rising to such occasions

SOUPS

Julienne   Mock Turtle

FISH

Cod   Turbot

JOINTS

Haunches of Venison
Sirloins of Beef   Rounds of Beef
Haunches of Mutton   Stewed Beef
Hashed Venison

POULTRY

Turkeys   Geese   Chicken

GAME

Pheasants   Partridges

ENTREMETS

Plum Puddings   Gateau de Pomme
Charlotte a la Russe   Normandy Pippins
Compote of Pears   Tipsy Cake

Wine and Marachino Cherries

DESSERT

The wines were supplied from Plymouth and were of the finest vintages, comprising port, sherry, champagne, hock and claret.

The hotel continued to run prestigious events in the ballroom and William Northway continued

Advert from the Tavistock Gazette of 22 December 1876

to run an excellent dining room. For a meeting of the Bedford Lodge of Freemasons No 282 on 5 January 1876

" ... the Bretheren adjourned to the Bedford Hotel, where a sumptuous banquet awaited them, provided by Bro. Northway, who on this as on all other occasions, proved himself an excellent caterer ... "

And a 'jolly' for the great and the good was run in Northway's establishment in the New Year of 1877; an event where many would likely bow and scrape and ingratiate themselves to the Tavistock worthies.

It would appear that architecturally over the years the hotel offered a pleasing aspect in the town of Tavistock. Rachel Evans, a local Victorian authoress, admired the building and its setting writing in her book Home Scenes of Tavistock and its Vicinity as early as 1846 liked the juxtaposition of hotel and abbey remains

"The chief hotel with embattled walls built of freestone raised on the place, is a fine structure, corresponding in all respects with the Abbey remains grouped around."

Whilst many important events took place during Northway's reign at the Bedford no documented major additions or subtractions to the Hotel have been found. However, a very early photograph from c1866 clearly shows the juxtaposition of the various portions of the Bedford Hotel site in that year and this 1860s photograph, likely taken from the top of the nearby tower of St Eustachius parish church is interesting for at least two important reasons. Firstly, it shows clearly the extent of the range of the two-storey stable block, to the south of the hotel. This block not only extends fully across the yard but turns north and occupies the site of what was later to become the hotel garage facility for the motoring visitors from the early 1900s until 1988. Secondly, assuming that the 1823 engraving of the newly-opened Bedford Hotel is an accurate representation of the hotel it is clear that a second floor has been added over the entrance and to the west.

The hotel had a good reputation, at least in the immediate neighbourhood, and in 1860 a local directory described it thus

" ... enter the Bedford Hotel where the stranger will find good entertainment for man and beast. This excellent inn was originally a private mansion but has been enlarged and elegantly fitted up for the accommodation of the public."

It was also considered as being architecturally impressive and Burritt in his book on his walk from London to Lands End and back in 1868 described the hotel thus

"The Bedford Hotel occupies part of the site of the old edifice and presents an aspect of antiquity – like a full size castle arising phoenix-like out over the ruins of a cathedral."

Bit over the top that.

View looking south from the tower of the parish church across the Bedford Hotel. The newly built GWR station of 1859 can be seen (top right) together with Deer Park Lodge (top middle) that was built in 1850. St.Johns House, which now stands to the right of the Lodge, was not built until the late 1860s.

As the hotel advertised a blue blood intention when it came to life in 1822 it is perhaps understandable that it continued to be the premier hotel during the tenancy of William Rowe Northway. By 1881 William Rowe was in his mid-seventies, and a widower, Sally having died in 1876 of 'softening of the liver and exhaustion'; whether the liver was antagonistic to alcoholic intake is not known. Their son William Rowe junior, born in Tavistock in 1844, assisted with the running of the hotel; he had married Lucy Jane Hooper in Plymouth in the spring of 1879 and was now the proud father of a son, William H G R Northway, born in 1880. To assist in the running of what must have been a busy hotel the live-in staff level had grown from seven in 1851 to eleven in 1881 when the staff are given as

Simon Webber	52	barman	born in Tavistock
Elizabeth Webber	52	barwoman	born in Peter Tavy
Mary New	50	barmaid	born in London
Jessie Snell	27	chambermaid	born in Brentor
Emma Lang	25	chambermaid	born in Maristow
Mary Kenner	22	kitchenmaid	born in Bere Ferrers
Annie Cole	21	nursemaid	born in Mary Tavy
Mary Sussex	28	waitress	born in Launceston
Mary Bailey	18	waitress	born in Tavistock
William Knight	51	boots	born in Tavistock
Thomas Dawe	25	underboots	born in Milton Abbot

Throughout the whole of the period 1841 to 1881 it is seen that the greater majority of the staff were local born. The standard of staff for the best hotel also needed to be up to the requirement of Victorian propriety as shown by an advertisement in the *Tavistock Gazette* in 1873 for probably the lowliest position in the hotel, that of underboots – "wanted, respectable, steady, industrious young man as underboots." Nevertheless at least some of the servants were loyal to the end and William Knight died in service in 1885, aged 56 after 36 years service in the hotel.

Both William Northway senior and junior were elected officers of the Freemasons' Bedford Lodge No 282 and the brethren were not averse to attending the odd 'sumptuous banquet' in the Bedford Hotel after the proceedings. Also William Rowe senior was not simply a man of business his philanthropic interests being seen in a number of ways. He sat on the Tavistock Board of Guardians and, on a more personal level, made personal contributions by, for example, his arranging a collection of £3 for the Exeter Fire Relief Fund, after 140 people lost their lives on 5 September 1887 when the New Theatre Royal in Exeter burnt down. The fact that the Mayor of Exeter was somewhat tardy in acknowledging such public spirit may have layed heavily with William and he died in the Bedford Hotel of bronchitis on 7 November 1887. Strangely for such an important local personage, no obituary appears in the *Tavistock Gazette* and the Death Notice simply states that he was to be interred at Chagford churchyard on 12 November and that the death notice would be the only public announcement of his passing. Sally and William Rowe senior lie together in Chagford parish churchyard, the Northways continuing to advertise, this time on their tombstone as

"In remembrance of S. Northway the beloved wife of W R Northway of the Bedford Hotel, Tavistock, died March 31st 1876 aged 70 years.

Also of the above W R Northway who died November 7th 1887 aged 79 years.

His end was peace

Mary Rowe Lee, daughter of the above died 10th March 1905 aged 68 years.

Her end was peace"

Although William Rowe Northway junior is named in his father's Will as an Hotel Proprietor it seems that William junior did not take on the tenancy of the Bedford but continued the Northway interest in farming and in 1891 lived in Handsworth, Glanville Road, Tavistock, which he had purchased in auction for £580 in April 1888. Before parting William arranged a tea for about 30 of his late employees and their guests, with all present expressing the sentiment that "Mr and Mrs Northway must enjoy health and happiness in their retirement", which sounded rather more like an instruction than a well wish. William Rowe Northway junior had, however, found time for other activities as well as helping to run a hotel – he played cricket for Tavistock Cricket Club from the 1850s through to the 1870s. He was only 43 when he retired to live at Handsworth with his wife Lucy, and in 1898 he became a founder member of the Tavistock Urban District Council, was re-elected in 1901 but lost his seat in 1902. The couple moved to St Columb in Cornwall some time after 1902 and Lucy died there in 1917 aged 61 and William in 1924 aged 80.

Despite William Rowe junior not continuing in the licensed trade the Northway family as a whole had made formidable commitment to Tavistock being licensed victuallers here for a total of one hundred and seventy nine man years over the period 1793 to 1888 – that's a lot of pints and a lot of 'sumptuous feasts'. The Northway adventure had, however, not been without its rewards along the way – William Rowe Northway senior left a net estate of £22984, equivalent to some £1.1 million today.

The new tenant was to be another Tavistock victualler, John Squire late of the Newmarket Hotel in Duke Street who took over the tenancy of the Bedford on 25 March 1888. Undoubtedly, Squire, like Northway before him, had to pass the tests of interview(s) with the Duke's Stewards. That John came from good stock was beyond question, his father Thomas having run a large farm at Smallacombe, South Brentor, for many years until his death in 1872 aged 66. Thomas and his wife Mary Stephens (nee Ellis) raised 7 children of whom John was welcomed as number four. Thomas Squire and Mary Stephens Ellis had married in Plymouth in 1846, Mary being the firstborn of a family of 11 children raised at Wortha Mill in Mary Tavy by the miller William Ellis and his wife Ann (nee Stephens). The Ellis family were eventually to become maltsters in Tavistock with very close connections with the licensed trade, having been lessees, over the period 1851 to 1871, of the Market House Inn, the Ordnance Arms and the New Market Inn. The Ellis family also had strong connections, through marriage, with the Squire family when in the mid 19th century at least three of the Ellis family girls married into the Squire family.

The land was not for our John. The local lad, born in South Brentor in Lamerton parish on 20th of August 1853, had run the New Market Inn in Duke Street, Tavistock, with his elder sister Annie (given names Anne Eliza), from the end of November 1876 when John was still only 23

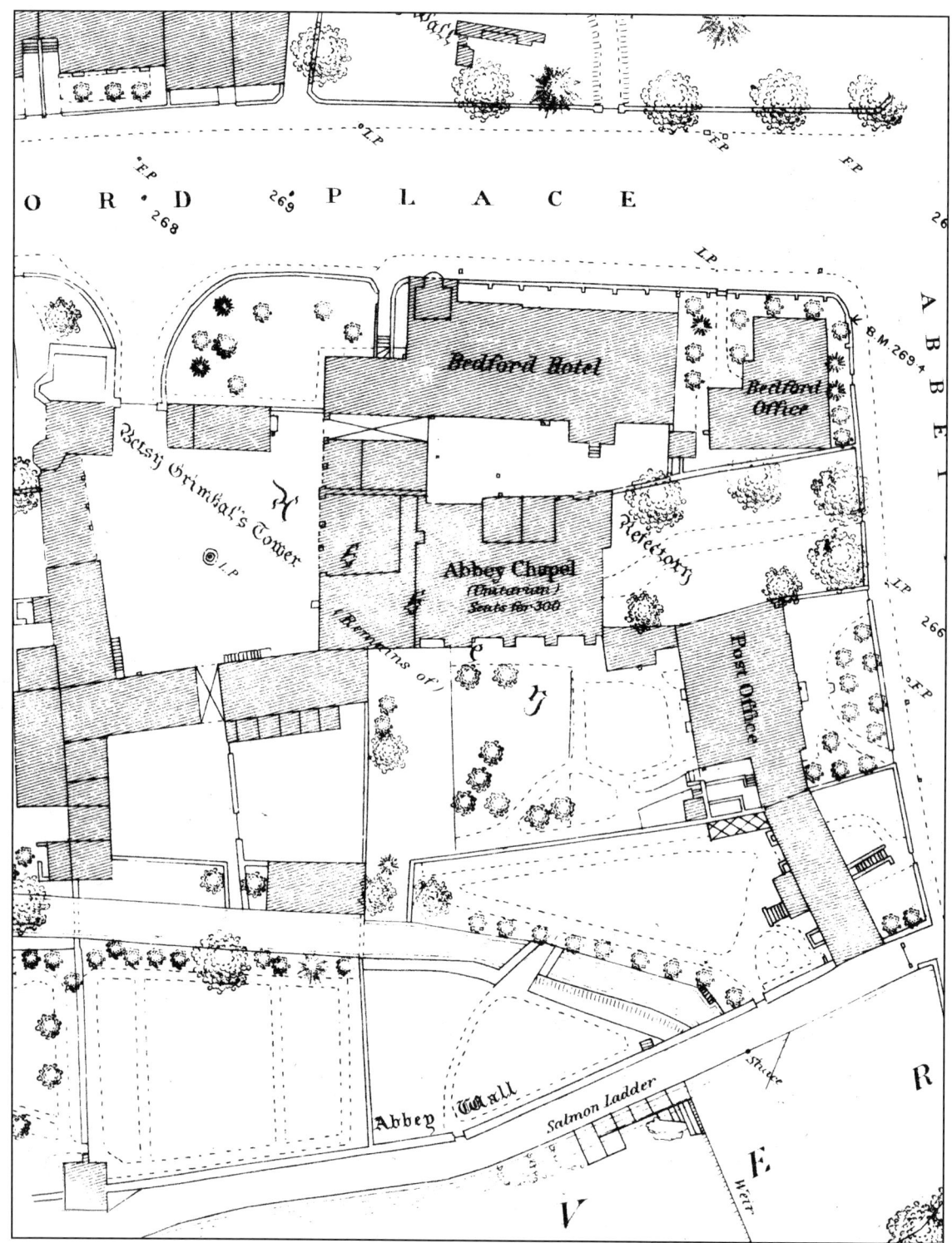

OS map   footprint of the Bedford Hotel site in 1883

years of age. He had, however, been 'hardened off' to life's trials losing his mother when he was 9 and his father at age 18. On his move upmarket to the Bedford Hotel in 1888 John was determined to make his mark. First he advertised his hotel in the *Tavistock Gazette*; on 13 April 1888 and 4 May the paper reported that

> "The Bedford Hotel is undergoing extensive alterations; in fact the internal parts are being entirely remodelled, modern appliances being introduced wherever possible even to the use of electric bells for the various rooms. Quite a little army of artisans is employed in order to expedite the works."

> "The furniture for the Bedford Hotel, which has been specially manufactured for the proprietor Mr John Squire, is now being exhibited at Plymouth by the makers Messrs Spooner and Co."

It is assumed that these renovations were undertaken with John Squire's own money, or that of his family.

John's next important step was to take unto himself a lawful wedded wife; on 19 November 1890, at St George's, Tufnell Park, Islington, he married Kate Lanham, born in Camden Town in 1858 and at the day of her wedding living at 184 Tufnell Park Row, in Islington. Kate had come from a victualling background, her father Joseph, over a period of some 25 years running, firstly, the Camden Arms in Camden Town followed by the Feathers in Hanover Square. Joseph had married a very young widow, Maria Bonham Hall (nee Crisp), who came with two small children from her previous marriage to a Harry Bonham Hall in 1847. Three years later Harry was dead and Maria was a widow aged 24 and a licensed victualler running the Camden Arms. Within fifteen months Maria was to marry Joseph Lanham who not only got a new wife but also a pub and two young step children – a bargain. Over the next five years four more little Lanhams joined the family, all this being a little too much for Maria who died in the summer of 1861 leaving Joseph with a pub, two stepchildren and four of his own, Kate being the youngest. Maria was only 34. On the death of Joseph in 1876 Kate's elder stepbrother William Hall ran the pub with Robert Lanham her brother; Kate and sister Maria were given as assistant housekeepers in the census of 1881.

Kate, like her John Squire husband to be, had lost her mother when she was only ten years old and her father when she was in her late teens. Both Kate and John had worked in inns with their siblings before they themselves married and ran a licensed house. Kate was to survive life's hardships better than her husband.

Some time after spring 1881 Kate Lanham had come to the New Market Hotel in Tavistock and met John; the *Tavistock Gazette* reported this date as early as 1878 when John Squire was living at Deerpark and was the proprietor of the New Market Hotel. The newspaper report also states that Kate was associated with the famous de Keyser Hotel by Blackfriars Bridge in London but this has not been confirmed, despite trying. John and Kate had both left marriage until comparatively late in life, John being 37 and Kate 32, perhaps because of their both having to survive at an early age without parental governance. However, to make up for lost time they had three children, Frank (Harry) in 1891, Emily in 1893 and Arthur in 1894. Emily died in infancy in 1893.

TAVISTOCK.

Valuable Brewery with extensive Bottle, Cask, and Spirit Trade, together with Two Freehold and Five Leasehold Licensed Houses, as a Going Concern.

Plan, Particulars and Conditions of Sale

Of the VERY VALUABLE and HIGHLY IMPORTANT FREEHOLD PROPERTY, known as

The TAVISTOCK BREWERY,

With Wholesale and Retail "Off" Licenses,

In the Town of Tavistock,

Comprising the well-fitted Brewery Premises, Offices, Stabling and Appurtenances, together with the adjoining FREEHOLD LICENSED PREMISES, known as

The TAVISTOCK HOTEL,

Situate in the Centre of Tavistock ;

Also the FREEHOLD FULLY-LICENSED PREMISES, known as

The "HARVEST HOME," Tavistock,

Together with LEASEHOLD INTERESTS in

The WHITE HART INN, Chilsworthy ;   PETERTAVY INN, Petertavy ;
The NEW INN, Horndon ;   ROYAL STANDARD INN, Marytavy ;
And Tied-Trade Interest in the FOREST INN, Hexworthy ;

With the benefit of the old-established and improved Free, Tied and Private Trade, the whole of which will be Sold as a going concern, with the Fixed Plant and Machinery, with possession on completion of the Purchase,

Which will be SOLD BY AUCTION by

MR. PERCY HEXTER,

At the BEDFORD HOTEL, TAVISTOCK,

On WEDNESDAY, JULY 2nd, 1913, at 3 o'clock for 3.30 p.m.,

Subject to the General Conditions of the Plymouth Incorporated Law Society, and to such other conditions as will then be read.

Plan, Printed Particulars and such Conditions of Sale may be obtained of the AUCTIONEER, Mr. PERCY HEXTER, 28, Gandy Street, Exeter ('Phone 354) ; at the place of Sale ; at the Brewery ; or of the Solicitor,

Mr. A. K. G. JOHNSTONE, Tavistock.

For purpose of Viewing, Motor-cars can be hired at Tavistock from Messrs. Backwell & Son, or Messrs. Morris & Son.

Advertisement for the sale of Tavistock Brewery at the Bedford Hotel in 1913

In the spring of 1881 Annie, John Squire's elder sister married Frederick W Mathews in the Fulham Registration District. Frederick was the son of Joseph Mathews, iron founder of Tavistock, and part of a very influential local family which may explain why Frederick seems to have repeatedly done a temporary disappearing act as he is not found in England at census 1881, 1891 or 1901 (although he had found time to marry Annie). Annie, a lonely wife, is found in Gulworthy in 1891 and helping her brother in the Bedford in 1901. After John Squire's death in 1904 Annie ran the Manor Hotel in Lydford for some 18 years with her sister-in-law Ann Cory Squire, widow of John Squire's younger brother William. Annie died in her sleep, aged 75, a widow, in 1925, and Ann Cory died two days later; they are buried side by side in Brentor Christchurch cemetery.

In 1896 John Squire was to become a founding shareholder, and most likely a director, in the newly incorporated Tavistock Brewery Company under the chairmanship of Archibald D Flower, of Flower's Brewery of Stratford-upon-Avon. This venture was dissolved in 1899 and the Tavistock Brewery was sold to Edwin Bullen Gilbert, the tied houses being sold separately. John Squire appears to have taken advantage of the company disassembly as he bought one of the tied houses, the Tavistock Hotel. This appears to have been purely an investment deal as he quickly sold on the hotel to Hicks's Brewery of St Austell. Somewhat ironically, the Tavistock Brewery properties, including the Tavistock Hotel which had both been investments by John Squire, were put up for sale at the Bedford Hotel in 1913, one of many such important local property sales which were undertaken at the hotel.

The town of Tavistock was praised by a writer who was staying at Squire's Bedford Hotel in 1896

> "Whatever it may be to the permanent residents here, it is simply a paradise to spend a holiday in. The natives (than whom there could not possibly be a more kindly, courteous, and obliging race on this sublunary sphere) are anxious and eager to tell or show you anything and everything of this beautiful place, of which they are so highly proud. Oh that we could all live in Tavistock. If the jaded and careworn businessmen of London knew more of this place there would not be a spare bed to be found from May to October."

Presumption would be in favour of John Squire running a good hotel at this date and, under his stewardship, the great and the good not only stayed in the hotel but the hotel ballroom continued to be the venue for local binges for the top-brass to celebrate. On the 30th of September 1896 at two o'clock a luncheon was held at the hotel following the formal opening of the Constitutional Club in Bedford Street on the corner with the newly opened Drake Road. The guests of honour included Sir Edward Clarke, MP for Plymouth and Conservative heavyweight, and Sir Roper Lethbridge, MP for Kensington North from 1885 until 1892 who was also an academic, civil servant in India and latterly leader of the Unionist cause in Okehampton. The Bedford Hotel rose to the occasion as described in the *Tavistock Gazette* of 2nd October.

> "The ball room was decorated with mirrors, drapery, and flowers, and presented an attractive appearance. The was a button-hole for each person. A large number of ladies attended. An excellent repast was well served under the personal supervision

of Mr J Squire. A string band stationed in the balcony played during the luncheon, and contributed a suitable selection as each toast was proposed. The Chairman (Mr Edred Marshall) was supported on his right by Sir Edward Clarke, who was loudly cheered on entering the room, and on his left by Sir Roper Lethbridge. Grace before meat was said by the Rev G D Symonds, rector of Coryton, and after meat by the Rev C H Taylor, vicar of Milton Abbot."

Likely the only 'downer' for this day of celebration was the teeth-gnashing annoyance that the local Conservative candidate, Col White-Thomson, had recently been defeated in the 1895 parliamentary elections.

It was in the tenancy of John Squire that the company founded by Francis Frith, the pioneering Victorian photographer, began visiting Tavistock as part of this commercial venture to produce images of towns and villages for Victorians to collect. Images from 1893 clearly show the structure of the hotel viewed from the northeast and northwest.

From the northeast the hotel shows no change from the aspect that would have been obvious in 1822 when the new Bedford Hotel opened its doors. What is interesting, however, is that the hotel used Frith images in a commercial manner and presented the same as postcards and the format, of address on one side of a standard size of card and picture on the other, dates from 1899. In 1902, what freedom, the sender was allowed to write message and address on the same side of the card leaving the reverse to sport a full size picture. The 1893 image card was still in

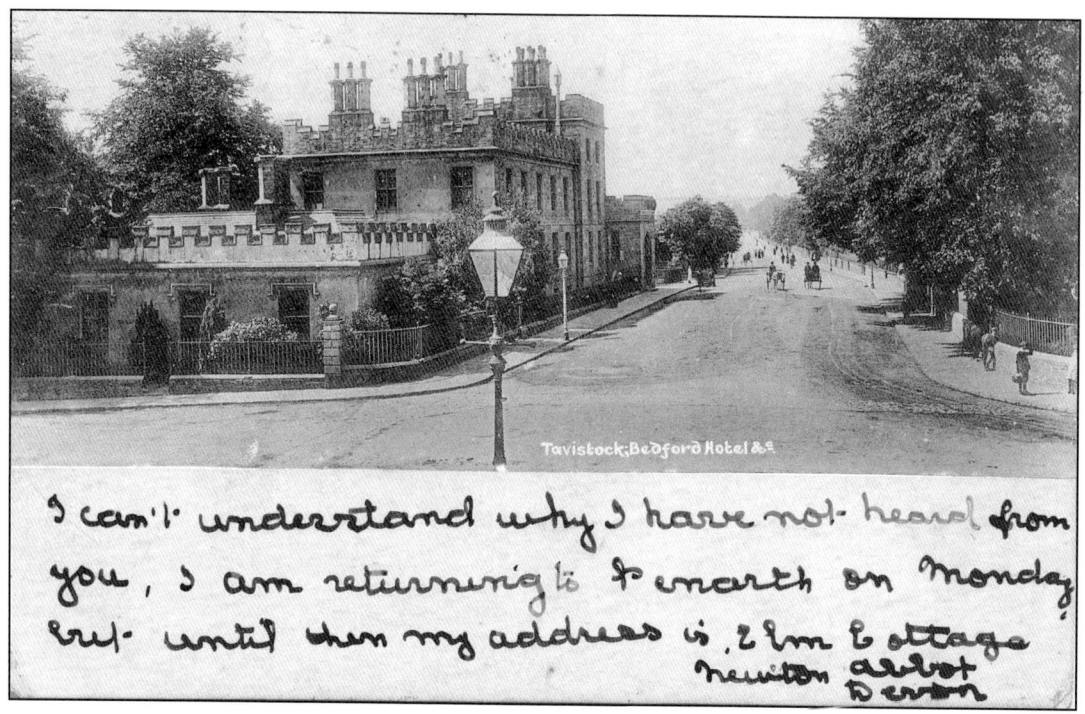

Postcard stamped 24 July 1901. This is a copy of an 1893 Frith image of the Bedford Hotel seen from the north-east. The card is an example of the written message being on the picture side of the card

Bedford Hotel from the north-west in 1893 clearly showing the ballroom long windows on the right

The Bedford Hotel from the north-east in 1898 – note the two gentlemen in front of the hotel

The Bedford Hotel from the north-east with car super-imposed some time in, or after, 1903
(unless the two standing gentlemen were glued in place for 5 years plus)

John Squire's Bedford Hotel showing two stages of development during the 'reign' of John Squire – the
addition of another two floors above the entrance porch and of the billiard room with the consequent
increase inheight of the wall running east to west to a height between ground and first floor windows.
The photograph also shows a rare glimpse of the stables in the yard with steps to upper level and
lamp standard on a plinth at the centre of the yard

An advertising card for Squire's Bedford Hotel postmarked 7 August 1905 and still being used after Squire's death in 1904

Northern elevation of the west end of the hotel in 2012 showing the ground floor of 1821, followed by the addition of floor 2 in 1830 followed by Squire's additional third floor c1900. Each floor is delineated by the differing stonework and had its own down pipe and header added at the time of building

use in 1923. In the 1893 image from the northwest the 1830 addition of the ballroom and second floor are clearly seen, plus two ladies going for a pint.

A later Frith edition dated 1898, taken from the north east, and a very similar view but with an early motor car is a wonderful surprise in that it shows that 'doctoring' of images was alive and well in the commercial world even then. The clue lies in the fact that the motor car has a licence plate (these were not introduced until 1903) but, unless the two gentlemen shown in the 1898 version had stood still outside the Bedford for 5 years plus, the motor car has been superimposed.

John Squire left his enduring mark on the Bedford Hotel being responsible for building, firstly, the upper floors at the west end of the hotel and, secondly, the addition of a billiard room, both completed before John's death in 1904. Access to the billiard room was via a new corridor formed at the north end of the ballroom reception area running part way as a raised level above the yard. The elaborate cornice of the reception area was maintained for all walls.

John Squire also had the privilege of taking the Bedford Hotel into the 20th century. What a night the 31st of December 1899 must have been yet, strangely, there is no local newspaper record of any celebratory event having taken place either in the Bedford or in Tavistock itself. The hotel had seen itself through sixty years of the reign of Queen Victoria through the great days of Empire and enterprise. The new century was to bring many technical achievements including the motor car. Whether it was John Squire who took the hotel into the motor age, or whether it was his successor, is not clear but by 1906, under the tenancy of Squire's successor, the hotel had moved on with the times and had its own facilities for motor cars as well as still retaining its stabling, which was situated at the south end of the ballroom, across the hotel yard.

Squire also celebrated both his upper floor addition and the introduction of photo postcards with his advertising card of c1905. This card also depicts two ladies going for a pint – perhaps the same two ladies as in the 1893 image?

John Squire died in the Bedford Hotel of acute pneumonia and asthenia (debility) on the 31st of August 1904 aged 51. A surprisingly short funeral report for a man who had contributed so much to Tavistock appeared in the *Tavistock Gazette* of 9 September and refers to the fact that John Squire was, at one time, a lieutenant in the Tavistock Detachment of the 2nd Volunteer Devonshire Regiment, a Past Master of the Bedford Lodge of Freemasons No 282 and a member of the Urban District Council. John left an estate of £7206 with a net personal estate of £5066, about half a million pounds in today's money.

As well as running a successful top country hotel John Squire undertook all those other duties with great diligence, being an inspiring leader to his men in the Volunteer Regiment and a major participant in Lodge and Council activities. John Squire's hotel and the local Volunteer Force honoured three members of the force returning from active service in the Boer War in South Africa. Volunteer Privates Parker, Hodge and Yard were welcomed by thousands on their arrival at Tavistock station and were "... entertained at dinner at the Bedford Hotel and heartily toasted ..." followed by a promenade concert attended by hundreds of people in the Market Hall. In Squire's year as Master of the Bedford Lodge in 1891 a conference of Freemasons from all over Devon met in his hotel. Here was a man seriously engaged in the business and politics of Tavistock. He also rode with the Sperling Hounds; in March 1895 he was unceremoniously dumped by his horse into the road at Portgate and was quite badly injured. It may perhaps have dulled the pain when he was moved to the pub in Portgate where he had to spend one or two weeks before returning to his home.

Sometime between 1893 and 1904 a third floor was added at the western end of the hotel. This addition is clearly seen in the above photographs and good evidence of the different floor additions is easily discernible on the northern elevation of the west end of the main part of the hotel today.

Kate outlived John, dying in Bath in 1933 at the age of 76; they share their last resting place in Plymouth Road Cemetery with their five-month old daughter Emily. Of their two sons Frank lived his life in Bath and Arthur at Mannabutts Tavistock.

John Squire's reign at the Bedford was to see the change from horse-drawn transport to the motor vehicle but the change was slow. Reginald Morshead, a direct descendant of Sir William Trelawny of Calstock and Patience Carpenter of Mount Tavy House in Tavistock, was a Devon County Councillor and business partner at Gill and Morshead, Bankers, of Tavistock. Phoebe Woollcombe, Reginald's granddaughter, describes Reginald's journey from Lamerton via Tavistock station to attend Council meetings

> "… the groom would drive him in to Tavi in the trap, then, having stabled the horse at the Bedford, would spend the day yarning in the pub 'til it was time to go back to the station for the master."

It would appear, therefore, that the Bedford stables were a commercial business not necessarily catering for wholly visitors to, or residents of, the hotel. However, there may well have been special arrangements for those 'in the know' and John Squire himself was noted as keeping 'fine horses' during his time at the Bedford. In addition, Hilary Davie, daughter of a local doctor Tom Davie, recalled that in the late 1940s a Hazel Ingold ran a riding school from the Bedford stables and Hilary would help with the stable duties and get free riding lessons.

In the same period of Squire's tenancy the ballroom was used for beginners, such as Phoebe's three aunts, as well as for accomplished dancers.

> "During the period 1890-1910 the young teenagers from all the big houses around would, once a week on Tuesdays, be driven in to the Bedford Hotel where a dancing teacher from Plymouth would take her class in the ballroom. The three girls from Hurlditch – my aunts – would go in the closed carriage and on the way home would be given a large piece of chocolate each as they were thought to be tired after their exertions on the dance floor! While the class was going on the horses would be unharnessed in the stables round the back and Phillips, the coachman, would sit yarning over his pipe with the other coachman."

According to the *Tavistock Gazette* "For years the house of Squire in the Tavistock District was associated with generosity – often enough – anonymously" and the successor(s) had a hard act to follow. John Squire had done well in life as did his three brothers; Thomas (1851-1929) was a well-known farmer at Brentor, Jonas (1855-1930) was a well-known local veterinary surgeon in Tavistock and William (1858-1930) was the manager at Messrs Pophams store in Plymouth.

Succession to the Squire tenancy of the Bedford Hotel, for a period covering the next 50 years was, again, in a similar manner to the Northway tenancy in Tavistock, to involve one family and its descendants. In addition, many of the forebears of the next 'generation' of Bedford tenants were involved in the pub and hotel trade and were also very closely involved with some of the great hotels of Plymouth and other towns. Enter the Stanbury family.

John Squire's immediate successor at Tavistock's premier hotel was a Mrs Ellen Stanbury. Ellen, nee Pearse, was the Totnes born widow of Samuel Downing Stanbury. Samuel had entered this world in Barnstaple as the sixth child of ten born to John Stanbury, a farmer and later farmer and auctioneer, farming at West Sowden, Barnstaple, in the mid nineteenth century. In his teens Samuel was a farm servant but on 26 January 1871, as a twenty seven year old master draper, he married Ellen Pearse, the daughter of Holne born farrier William Pearse, in the parish church of St George in Hanover Square in London. St George's was an Anglican church built in the early 1720s, to the design of John James, which became a fashionable place for marriages for the 'notable' set yet geographically and socially why a farmer's son from Barnstaple and a Totnes born daughter of a blacksmith from Holne on Dartmoor were married at St George's seems hard to explain.

The young Stanburys set up their home in Bridge Street in Leatherhead where, until at least 1878, Samuel had a business as an outfitter and linen draper and where their first child, Eva, was born in the summer of 1872. Next was a move into the licensed trade as by 1879 the Stanbury family had moved on to run the White Hart Hotel in the High Street in Brentwood, Essex, which was, again, to be an interim step. Sometime between 1881 and 1883 the Stanbury family moved to take over the White Hart Hotel in Okehampton where, on 30 July 1884, Samuel, licensed victualler, died of phthisis (TB) at the young age of 40: his sister Emily Elizabeth Castle was at his side.

Kelly's Directory for 1883 gives Samuel Downing Stanbury as 'mine host' in the White Hart in Okehampton having taken over from Tavistock born John Ball who had run this hotel for some 30 years. Ellen was left a widow at the age of 38 with two surviving children out of four. What had modelled the career pathway of Samuel Stanbury is not known but certainly the move into the licensed trade was to be a not uncommon career for the Barnstaple born children of John and Elizabeth Stanbury.

The early 1880s had not been very kind to Ellen Stanbury; in mid 1883 her son George Castle Stanbury was to die in Southampton district aged but one year old; in late 1883 her father-in-law, John Stanbury, aged 74, died in Heavitree Exeter; on 30 July 1884 her husband Samuel was to die in the White Hart Hotel in Okehampton and is buried in Okehampton parish churchyard; and then, in 1886, Samuel's mother, Elizabeth, sometimes Betsy, was to die in Bridge Street in Leatherhead, likely the ex-home of Samuel and Ellen in the 1870s but in 1886 the home of

*Samuel Downing
Stanbury (1844-1884)*

*Ellen Stanbury (1845-1910)
– lessee of the Bedford
Hotel from 1904 to 1910*

Samuel's sister Mary and her second husband John Shoolbred, draper. Ellen's husband Samuel had left a relatively small gross estate of £2206 with a net value of nil and now Ellen was on her own. However, from the death of Samuel the business life of Ellen Stanbury was to be in high-grade hotels in Plymouth and Tavistock. By 1888, following on from the loss of her husband, Ellen Stanbury had settled in as the proprietor of Chubb's Hotel at 8/9 Old Town Street in Plymouth.

The reason for Ellen's settlement in Plymouth after Samuel's death in Okehampton in 1884 is very possibly that Ellen, nee Pearse, had a much closer link both to the licensed trade in general and to Plymouth in particular, than may appear at first glance. The Royal Hotel in Plymouth's Athenaeum Street, built by John Foulston c1812 with the Athenaeum Theatre next door, was substantial and, according to Murray's Handbook of 1859, it could accommodate 'an army', it comprised more than fifty bedrooms and offered a large ballroom with a fine decorated ceiling – the place to stay for people of substance. From at least 1844 this hotel was run by William Edwin Elliott, with his wife Anne, nee Webber, likely until his death in Plympton in 1867 when the hotel came under the hand of Samuel Pearse: coincidentally William Edwin Elliott's father had run the Royal Hotel in Devonport together with a coachbuilding business. The possible inter-family business connections here are interesting.

Without doubt there is an established link of the Royal Hotel in Plymouth and the Bedford Hotel in Tavistock through William Edwin Elliott. William Edwin was the brother of Edmund Lakeman Elliott, lessee of the Bedford Hotel through the 1840s until the death of his other brother, Thomas, in 1850 with Edmund then taking over the coachbuilding interests of the Elliott family in Devonport. William Edwin Elliott's tenure of the Royal in Plymouth likely ended with his death in 1867 and by 1871 Samuel Pearse was in charge. The surname Pearse is cause enough to consider a possible link with Ellen Stanbury nee Pearse but the fact that Samuel Pearse had married a Margaret Stanbury in Exeter in 1849 is enough to make any genealogist salivate with anticipation. To date the clincher for a family link between Samuel Pearse and Ellen Stanbury nee Pearse has not yet been found but that such a link exists seems a strong possibility and, moreover, what does appear to be true is that the broader Stanbury family still had connections with the Royal Hotel into the 1940s; this was despite Samuel losing the lease at auction in 1869 but somehow regaining control until 1903.

It may, however, simply have been Ellen Stanbury's business dealings with Chubb's Hotel that led to the eventual business arrangement with the Bedford Hotel as the Chubb's and the Northways of the Bedford Hotel were related through marriage. In 1888 Ann Chubb the proprietor of Chubb's Hotel died. Ann was the widow of Francis Henry Chubb, Tavistock born farmer's son, who had named Chubb's in Old Town Street sometime between 1851 and 1861, renaming the Commercial Hotel that he had run since at least 1850. Francis married Tavistock born Ann Northway in 1844, Ann's uncle being William Rowe Northway, tenant of the Bedford from 1850 to his death in 1887 – oh, what a tangled web they weave.

Ellen Stanbury appears to have owned and run Chubb's Hotel from 1888 when she held an inaugural complimentary dinner at Chubb's on 9 May 1888 surrounded by many 'habitues of the hotel'. These included J H Stanbury, Ellen's brother-in-law of Exeter; Tavistock born Frank Chubb, late owner of Chubb's Hotel and widower of Ann, nee Northway, Chubb; John Jackman of Tavistock who had married a Mary Northway, grand-daughter of William Northway, and also Frank Ward, well-known estate agent and surveyor of Tavistock whose aunt was a Mary Northway. At complimentary dinners guests all say nice things about the host and Ellen's guests were no less gracious, Mr Frank Chubb proposing "The Health of the Hostess – whose kind deeds and actions, done in a simple and unostentatious way were well known." Alderman Newcombe, ex-Mayor of Okehampton considered that those who frequented the hotel might consider themselves fortunate that they had such an excellent lady as Mrs Stanbury to succeed Mrs Chubb: all in all lots of applause for Ellen Stanbury. Chubb's Hotel itself also received plaudits being described as a hotel that was a household word throughout the country and the colonies.

In the spring of 1891 Ellen was living at Chubb's Hotel with her two surviving daughters and her niece Amy Stanbury, daughter of her brother-in-law John Headon Stanbury. Two years later Ellen was to be joined on a more permanent basis in Plymouth by her brother-in-law who had bought the Grand Hotel on Plymouth Hoe. John had been an hotel keeper since 1881 and he was living in Exeter up to 1893, which was probably the year he took on the Grand in Plymouth. He had been running the Half Moon hotel and posting house in Exeter, together with the Tap and a wine and spirit merchants in Martin Street. By 1897 John was still responsible for the Half Moon in Exeter as well as the Grand Hotel in Plymouth, both of which were high-class establishments. The Grand Hotel, built in 1878 on the Hoe in Plymouth, was no mean establishment boasting some 40 bedrooms and supporting facilities and, employing some 11 staff in 1881 rising to 23 staff in 1891.

Ellen Stanbury was at the Chubb's Hotel until at least 1896 and likely until 1898 when the hotel was purchased by Messrs G Shellabear and Sons for £35000. By 1901 Ellen had moved on to the Central Hotel in Lockyer Street and in 1904 had also taken the Bedford Hotel, Tavistock, under her wing. What precipitated Ellen's moves is not known but in 1903 John Headon Stanbury had sold the Grand Hotel for £57400 and, also in that year, the United Plymouth Hotels Ltd company was formed; the company prospectus described five hotels which were to form the group including the Grand, the Royal and Chubb's Hotel, all previously having connections with Stanbury and or Pearse families. Perhaps this latter business venture was a move too far as in 1908 the United Plymouth Hotels company was wound up and the Investors' Review of 4 July 1903 appears to have been correct when it reported, when reviewing the proposed merger, that "We do not like the thing much, and it must not be forgotten that the P and O steamers are going to cease calling at Plymouth."

Whilst keeping her interests in the Central Hotel in Plymouth, Ellen Stanbury ran the Bedford Hotel until her death from cardiac failure on 17 January 1910 aged 64.

During at least part of the period of Ellen Stanbury's tenure of the Bedford the chef was a local lady, Mrs Emma Jane Rogers, wife of local monumental mason, John Giles Rogers. Emma Jane was likely instrumental in securing work at the hotel for her son Reginald Harry Rogers, who was a notable 'short stay' worker and who, after serving with the Rev Maitland Kelly at Kelly House, had a brief spell in the Bedford Hotel before working for three years as an assistant waiter at the Angel Hotel, Helston. In 1912 Harry, as he was known to his friends, decided to better himself and emigrate to America and stay, firstly, with his uncle and aunt at Wilkes Barre in Pennsylvania. His berth to America was transferred to the Titanic because of a coal strike and

The Grand Hotel, Plymouth, in 1904 (copyright Plymouth Museum)

Chubb's Hotel, Plymouth, in 1904 (copyright Plymouth Museum)

Emma Jane Rogers – chef at the Bedford Hotel c1908

Harry Rogers – Bedford Hotel worker and Titanic victim

Harry was one of the 1514 passengers who lost their lives when the liner went down on its maiden voyage.

During her time at the hotel Ellen Stanbury appears not to have made any substantial changes to the fabric or facilities offered by the hotel. She had, however, used postcards as advertising material but strangely chose to use line engravings showing horse transport whilst there is no doubt that in her 'reign' motor car facilities appeared in the Bedford offering. Kelly's Directory of 1906 described the virtues of the Bedford as

> "Bedford family and commercial hotel, completely redecorated and up to date, posting in all its branches; splendid hunting; fishing and golf in district; large loose boxes for hunters; motor garage, pit and petrol."

Who ran the garage facilities in the early days is not clear but by 1930 John Backwell had established his business as the Bedford Hotel Garage with motor cars on hire day and night, lock-up garages, oil, petrol etc. This first appearance of Backwells in the Bedford Hotel Garage coincides with the withdrawal of the Backwell waggonette service in June 1930 to make way for a chauffeur driven car service. Strangely, Backwell was not mentioned in this capacity at the Bedford in 1939 but was only listed as running the Bedford Hotel Riding Stables, a business which had also been mentioned in 1935 alongside the Garage. Whatever Backwell's involvement garage facilities at the Bedford Hotel yard were extant up to their closure on 18 April 1988 when the premises were "required for future development". From 1982 the garage was rented by Dennis Carr from Trust Houses and was run on a day-to-day basis by his son Ian until its closure. The garage sold Shell petrol and undertook minor repairs. The buildings that comprised the motor garage service, which were situated on the western side of the hotel yard, were not demolished until 2000.

Although Ellen Stanbury's tenure of the Bedford Hotel was a relatively short six years the Stanbury family were not bowing out of the hotel so easily. Somewhere along the way Florence Mary, Ellen's daughter, had met a young man in his mid twenties, William Isaac Lake. They married in Plymouth in the autumn of 1897.

Lake had come from brewing stock. His father Isaac was born in Romford and became a brewery foreman, manager, storekeeper and finally, in 1911, hotel proprietor of the Royal Hotel, Bodmin. Isaac married Ellen Rowley Collier, also from Romford, in the summer of 1867 and raised at least three surviving children of which William Isaac, born in the autumn of 1870 in Romford, was the eldest. William also went into the brewery trade and became a travelling salesman for Ind Coope and later for the wine merchants John Hawker. In the 1890s Ind Coope had an office in at 6 Old Town Street, Plymouth, more or less next to Chubb's Hotel, and by 1896 William Isaac Lake was the manager, no doubt in commercial contact with Mrs Stanbury at the hotel and it is not difficult to see how William and Florence Stanbury met. He was soon in partnership with Mrs Stanbury in the Central Hotel, in Lockyer Street, Plymouth and from 1910 William was licensee of the Lockyer Hotel, a licence that he held with Walter Cooper until 1927. On the death of Ellen Stanbury in 1910 the Central Hotel continued under the ownership of Stanbury and Co until it closed c1938. In 1910 the hotel was valued by the Inland Revenue at £11000, about half that of the Grand Hotel in Elliott Street. The occupiers of the Central Hotel at that

The Lockyer Tavern, Lockyer Street, Plymouth pictured in the 1950s. The hotel licence was held by William Isaac Lake 1910-1927

*William Isaac Lake
(1870-1955),
lessee of the Bedford Hotel
1910-1955*

*Florence Mary Lake
(1874-1934),
daughter of Ellen Stanbury*

date are given as Florence Mary Lake and Eva Ellen Dobell, Florence's sister ie Ellen Stanbury's two daughters. At the same review of Duties on Land Values for Tavistock the Bedford Hotel was valued at £7500. The Gross Values of the two hotels for Revenue purposes also roughly represent the rooms available in each in 1934 viz 40 at the Central Hotel and 30 in the Bedford. Strangely, however, a night's Bed and Breakfast in the Bedford was roughly 11 shillings per night compared to 10 shillings in the Central Hotel, both being a cut above the many.

At the time of the death of his mother-in-law in 1910 William Lake was still working as a commercial traveller but henceforth he took over the Bedford Hotel in partnership with his wife and they lived in Tavistock from 1910 to 1919 with their two daughters Doris and Margaret. At the 1911 census the return shows William, wife and two daughters in residence with one visitor, a governess for the two girls aged 12 and 8, 12 servants and three boarders. Frederick William Tucker and his wife, Susan, both aged 44 and from Plymouth, were the attendants in the Tap. Lake and his wife did not continue to live in the hotel but commuted Tuesdays and Fridays from Plymouth where, according to Sheila Stoneman, a long serving employee of the Bedford Hotel starting in William Lake's 'day', he is said to have run a hotel in Plymouth.

William and Florence Lake were not struggling for money when they took over the Bedford. In her Will proven in Exeter in February 1910 Ellen left a Gross Estate of £15674, equivalent to some £900,000 today, and a net personal estate of £4653. Apart from a weekly payment of £1 a week for life to her son John Pearse Stanbury Ellen bequeathed her estate to be divided equally between her two daughters. Ellen appears from her Will to have gone to some length to ensure strict control of the legacy to her son demonstrating almost a mistrust of his potential actions. John Pearse Stanbury had not followed into the hotels business in Plymouth and had become a caterer in London, associated with the Masons. He died in Plymouth, seemingly without issue, in the winter of 1920.

By 1905 the footprint of the hotel and grounds had changed little from that of sixty years previously but Lake was to make many changes to the hotel during his tenancy and added the veranda on the north side of the billiard room at some time between 1910 and 1916, likely in 1912. This veranda was then accessed internally by the corridor leading to the billiard room but had its own entrance – the chaps playing billiards could not be disturbed.

Lake was to show off the veranda on his advertising postcards but until that time he frugally used up his mother-in law's old stock. Strangely Ellen had chosen to use a line engraved illustration of the hotel and William, again with an eye to saving money, simply had his new veranda engraved on the Ellen Stanbury plate which was used as a letterhead.. These engraved images of the hotel were used as letterheads during the relevant occupations. William Lake was also responsible for the conversion of Foulston's Ball Room, aka Assembly Rooms, into more bedrooms some time within the period 1930 to 1933. This conversion lost the town a useful and historic public meeting place for social and political events. Thankfully, however, the ceiling plasterwork of the Ball Room was not totally destroyed and some clear examples can still be seen in the upper floor bedrooms of the west, rear wing of the hotel.

Notwithstanding whether William Lake resided full time in the hotel normal activities seem to have continued with the hotel catering for local sales etc and the hotel appears to have been

CENSUS OF ENGLAND AND WALES, 1911.

Large Schedule, with space for 40 names.

Number of Schedule. (To be filled up by the Enumerator after collection.)

Before writing on this Schedule please read the Examples and the Instructions given on the back of page 2, as well as the headings of the Columns. The returns are not to be used for proof of age, as in connection with Old Age Pensions, or for any other purpose than the preparation of Statistical Tables.

The contents of the Schedule will be treated as confidential. Strict care will be taken that no information is disclosed with regard to individual persons. The entries should be written in Ink.

NAME AND SURNAME	RELATIONSHIP to Head of Family.	AGE (last Birthday) and SEX.		PARTICULARS as to MARRIAGE.					PROFESSION or OCCUPATION				BIRTHPLACE	NATIONALITY	INFIRMITY.
		Ages of Males.	Ages of Females.	Write "Single," "Married," "Widower," or "Widow,"	Completed years the present Marriage has lasted	Total Children Born Alive.	Children still Living.	Children who have Died.	Personal Occupation.	Industry or Service	Employer/Worker/Own Account	Working at Home			
1 Lake William Isaac	Head	40		Married	13				Hotel Proprietor		Employer		Romford Essex	116	
2 Lake Florence Mary	Wife		36	Married	13	2	2						Lackenheath Surrey	90	
3 Lake Doris Mary	Daughter		12										Plymouth Devon	153	
4 Lake Margaret Ethel	Daughter		8										Romford Devon	151	
5 Gandy Kathleen F.?	Visitor		24	Single					Governess	443	0		Brompton	151	
6 Payne Alice Eliza	Servant		36	Single					Housekeeper (Hotel)	641	Worker		H. Chidcock Dorset	360	
7 Ruffell Amy	Servant		34	Single					Kitchenmaid (Hotel)	850	Worker		Kingston Thames	190	
8 Twelves Fred'k William	Servant	44		Widower	19	1		1	Barman (Hotel)	946	Worker		Stonehouse Devon	
9 Twelves Susan Agnes	Servant		44	Married	19	2	1	1	Barmaid (Hotel)		Worker		Plymouth Devon	153	
10 Irwin Bessie	Servant		25	Single					Waitress (Hotel)	943	Worker		Camborne Cornwall	370	
11 Mulroney Bertha Ann	Servant		23	Single					Chambermaid (Hotel)	641	Worker		Plymouth Devon	153	
12 McCoy Kitty	Servant		27	Single					Pantrymaid (Hotel)		Worker		Co Mayo Ireland	642	
13 Coval Arthur	Servant	19		Single					Billiard Marker (Hotel)	462	Worker		Alexandria Egypt	681	
14 Bradley Herman May	Servant		16	Single					Waiton Parle (Hotel)	44	Worker		Stonehouse Devon	
15 Shaddock Isabella	Servant		50	Widow					Cook (Hotel)	698	Worker		Kensington London	600	
16 Mooney Lily Elizabeth	Servant		23	Single					Kitchenmaid (Hotel)	641	Worker		Holloway London	
17 Crockett Ethel	Servant		22	Single					Laundrymaid (Hotel)		Worker		Devonport Devon	151	
18 Gillies Hunter Scott	Boarder			Single					Private house					
19 McLean Joseph Alexander	Boarder	63		Single					Retired Wholesale Draper	350	260		Manchester Lancashire	659	
20 Price Elish Blanche	Boarder		63	Widow									Langley Scotland	507	

To be filled up by the Enumerator.

Total to be carried forward to foot of page 2 ...

	MALES.	FEMALES.	PERSONS.
	6	14	20

[Continued on page 2.]

The 1911 census return for the Bedford Hotel

The Ellen Stanbury line-engraved postcard which William Lake continued to use

William Lake's line-engraved letterhead with the addition of the veranda – used in 1923

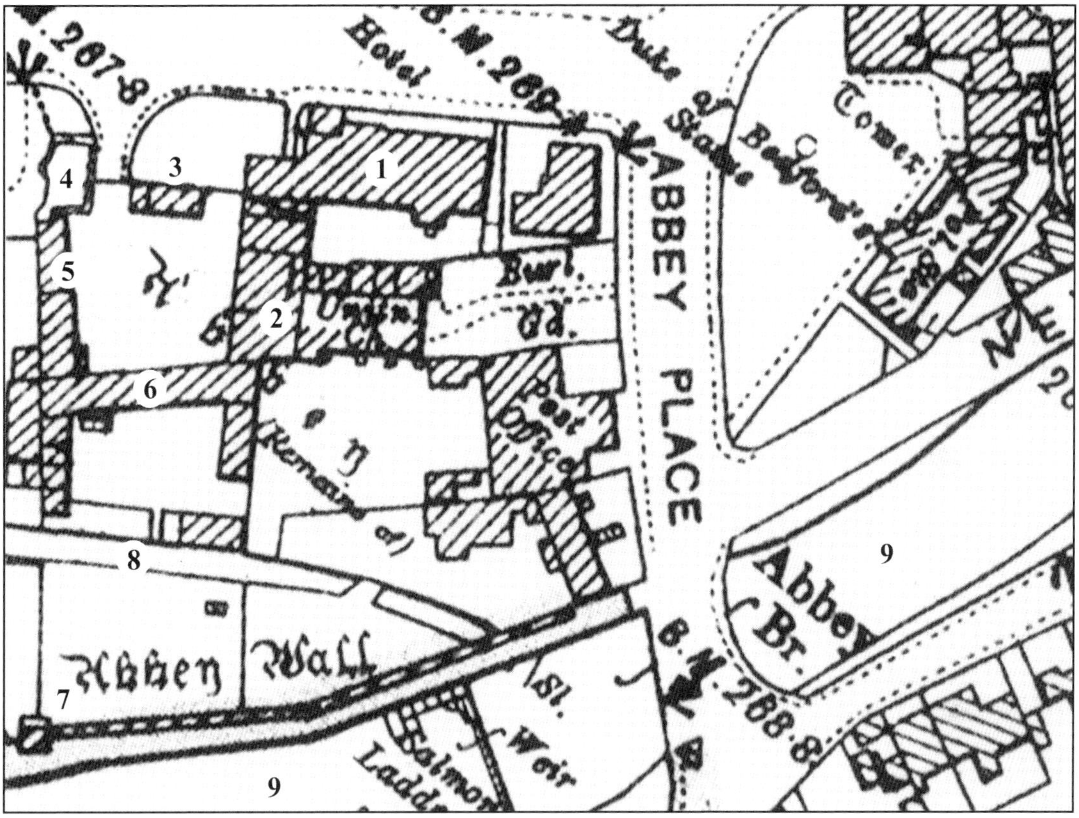

Footprint of the Bedford Hotel from OS Map 1905
1 – main hotel block, 2 – ballroom, 3 – billiard room, 4 – Betsy Grimbal's Tower, 5 – garage
6 – stable block, 7 – Still Tower, 8 – Tavistock Canal, 9 – River Tavy

The Bedford Hotel from the north-west showing Lake's new billiard room veranda c1920

more than 'agreeable' for residents and one resident wrote to his/her mother expressing satisfaction and future plans, possibly plans as part of a motoring holiday. The message is undated but is likely somewhere between 1903 and 1918

> "Darling mother. – ... This is a view from (our hotel) the other side and you dont see quite all of the building. It is such a nice hotel I dont know how we are going to leave it. But we go on to Cornwall next week not quite decided where yet and then perhaps back here again, then London and then to the lake district for a week or so before we finally return to "Eastwood". But I will keep you posted as to our address. The weather has ... "

Visits to the Bedford by true royalty have been hard to find although those who considered themselves royalty were likely many and boring. However, the Prince of Wales did make a fleeting visit to the hotel during his visit on 25 May 1921. Before entering the hotel the Prince inspected a guard of honour of the 5th Devon Cadets under Captain Alexander, headmaster of Tavistock Grammar School, and he used the hotel facilities to change his outfit from military uniform, worn for his presentation ceremony at Kelly College, to 'civvies' for his visit to the Devon County Show at Crowndale. The hotel made the best of the occasion with a large crown above the entrance and the usual polite 'yes sir, no sir' and likely milked the visit for a long time following. Some 16 years later, to commemorate the impending coronation of Edward VIII, William Isaac Lake issued complimentary notebooks as souvenirs of the expected event.

Little is known about the hotel activities in Lake's time but the hotel continued to be a venue for local sales etc. Lake also used the hotel as a touring centre and was not shy in business, describing the hotel in Kelly's Directory in 1939 thus –

> "Bedford Hotel ... (first class family); finest centre for motorists touring Devon and Cornwall ... excellent golf – 18 holes; hunting – 4 packs; salmon and trout fishing; tennis, croquet etc. Delightful scenery; real home comforts; best English catering; no chilled or foreign meats used; vegetables from own gardens; reduced terms October to Easter; hot and cold water in every bedroom; central heating; fully licensed; phone 37; moderate tariff ... "

The sourcing of local fresh produce is a theme which has been practised and advertised by a number of the managers of the hotel and the Bedford Hotel establishment was not just any hotel – it was a cut above the rest and such was exemplified by a local observer writing in the local paper about the Bedford as it was in the 1920s

> " ... only the 'Country Set' could use the Bedford Hotel in those days and guests dressed for dinner, but all that is in the past now."

Florence Mary Lake, William's wife, died at their Plymouth home at 7 Western College Road in May 1934 and William was later to marry again at the sprightly age of 70, to 47 year-old spinster Agnes Yorke. They married in St Luke's Church, South Lyncombe in Bath Borough.

Doris Lake, William's elder daughter, married Reginald Sansom White in St Andrews Church

Prince of Wales leaving the Bedford Hotel to attend the Devon County Show at Crowndale
25 May 1921

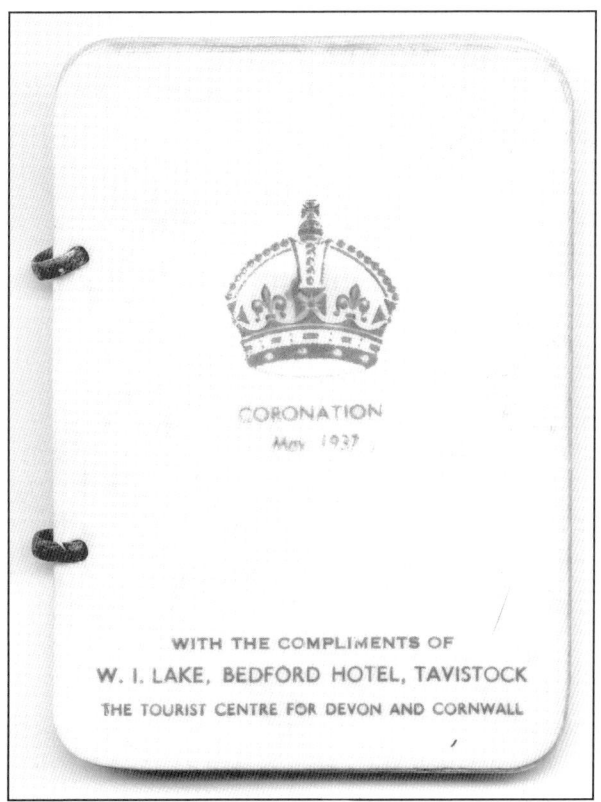

Complimentary souvenir notebook issued by William Isaac Lake
to commemorate the greatest non-event of 1937

Reginald and Doris Sansom White, the last managers of the Bedford Hotel before its sale in 1955

in Plymouth on 11 June 1924, the reception being held at the home of William Lake at Calumet, Western College Road, Plymouth, the bride and groom leaving on a 'honeymoon motor tour'. Doris's residence was given as the Central Hotel, Plymouth – grooming perhaps for her future career in Tavistock as manager, with her husband, of the Bedford Hotel which they managed for William Lake until the hotel's sale in 1955. Immediately following their wedding the Sansom Whites lived in Exeter for two years before moving to the Bedford in 1926.

Reginald Sansom White, born in Exeter in 1890, was the second son of John White, a poulterer, fish and game dealer, and his wife Mary both of whom were Exeter born and bred. Before appearing in Plymouth to woo Doris Lake Reginald had been a schoolteacher in Surrey in 1911. At the time of the wedding in 1924 he was given as a tradesman of Velwell Road, Exeter, perhaps taking over his father's business after the latter's death in Exeter in 1912 aged 49.

William Lake's younger daughter, Margaret, born in Plymouth in 1902, appears not to have had any involvement in the running of the Bedford. She had married a Capt James Kerr at St Andrew's Church in Plymouth on 27 November 1939, and in 1958 she was living in Lapworth in Warwickshire.

In 1937 a group of local worthies formed the Churchwardens' Pipe Smoking Union that first met in the Smoking Room which was situated immediately next to the Reception Desk toward the back of the hotel; strictly men only. In later years the Smoking Room became an office for the hotel administration and this group met in the west end of the main restaurant, smoked churchwardens' clay pipes and generally appear to have had a good time. This quirky association continued using the Bedford Hotel until moving to the local West Devon Club in the early years of the twenty first century and no doubt have lodged an appeal against the ban on smoking in public buildings and inns.

The Bedford Hotel, like other businesses, would have suffered the deprivations of the war years 1939-1945 and certainly there were the obvious restrictions, some causing the occasional problem. In August 1940 William Lake was fined for allowing a show of light during darkness from six bedrooms and a downstairs room. Lake pleaded that he had done all he could at considerable expense to blackout over 140 windows and skylights. The situation appears to have made William Lake somewhat grumpy as he stated that "An aeroplane would have to be coming along almost at street level to see it"; today he would, perhaps, have added "Mr Mainwaring". The Chairman of the Bench was extremely sympathetic – guilty; fined £2; next please!

Whilst William Lake was said to have been a stern man, his daughter Doris and her husband Reginald White were seemingly more affable and were well liked by their staff in Tavistock, where they were known as Sansom White rather than just plain White. According to long-serving employee Sheila Stoneman, who worked at the Bedford for over forty years from 1944, the hotel had 'very much a family atmosphere' under the new managers, Mr and Mrs Sansom White who lived in with their two children, the staff being treated as 'part of the family'. However, whilst the Sansom Whites were nominally in charge it would appear that William Lake kept a very close eye on things and many decisions which should, rightly, be left to the managers took up to two weeks to be verified by Mr Lake before they could be actioned.

The number of servants/non-managerial staff for the hotel seems to have stayed steady at 11 to 12 through the period 1881 to 1944. In 1944 the staff complement was 12, plus the two managers.

Managers	Mr and Mrs Sansom White
Housekeeper	Mrs Edna Cruikshank (known as Crooky)
Reception	Mrs Williamson
Chef	Mrs Greenaway
Kitchen maids	Susie ??; Sheila Stoneman
Chambermaid	Ruth ??
Dining Room	Mr Yelland
Gardener	Mr Charlie Doidge
Tap	Mr Slatter
Boilerman	Bill Chave
Boots/Porter	Alfred John Ham
Barman	?? Williams

In the war years also there was a restriction on what victuallers could charge for billeting soldiers. The going rate was 1/6d, 8p in today's money, for Bed and Breakfast for a soldier and 3/8d (18p) for an officer. It is thought unlikely that the Bedford advertised vacancies. However, it is known that the guests in 1944, for example, were mainly evacuees although it is not known who paid the bill.

Local girl Hilary Davie recalls that in the late 1940s the head waiter, Mr Yelland, was 'ancient and been there for years' and was all the more noticeable in the fact that 'he shuffled in to the restaurant to deliver the brown Windsor Soup, which was awful'.

Sheila Stoneman, a local Tavistock girl, joined the staff of the hotel in November 1944 as a kitchenmaid at the age of 14 at a wage of 10/- (50p) a week. As she was so young on starting she only worked from eight in the morning until 2.30pm. Her ambition was to become a cook, an ambition unfulfilled and Sheila was to work in the stillroom (tea and coffee only), for 5 to 6 years, and in the dining room. She eventually became a chambermaid, a post which she still held in 1988 when, with other long-serving employees of Trust House Forte, Sheila enjoyed a break at the Berystede Hotel in Ascot to commemorate her 44 years of service and was also offered a free week's holiday for two in the UK or Europe.

Such periods of long service at the Bedford were not unusual as with William Knight and the Northways in the nineteenth century. Alfred John Ham, porter and boots in 1944 worked in the hotel until he was well over 70. Alfred, known as John in the Bedford, was born in Launceston, trained as a saddlemaker but went to work for Plymouth's Chubb's Hotel which had been run by Ellen Stanbury, William Isaac Lake's mother-in-law. In 1897 Alfred somehow found his way to the Bedford Hotel, under John Squire, where he served for over 52 years including the period when Ellen Stanbury came to the Bedford. Alfred John Ham was considered to be the senior amongst the lower staff and always sat at the top of the table in the staff room. According to Trevor James Mr Ham, was a cheerful individual who always wore smart dark trousers and starched white jacket. He was a committee member of the Old Folks Rest Room in Tavistock and died in October 1955 at the age of 82 – rest well faithful servant.

There were/are other long serving members of staff at the hotel. The Slatters ran the Bedford Tap for 33 years; the Sansom White husband and wife team were managers for 30 years; Charlie Doidge tended the hotel gardens for more than 30 years and as late as 1985 porter Ron Taverner retired after 30 years of service. David Gee, who was born in Tavistock in 1957, joined the Bedford in 1974 and is still going strong as room manager in 2012 – he could win the longest-term service prize yet.

In 1944 the managers, the Sansom Whites, and their children Anthony and Margaret lived on the top floor and had a 'gorgeous' private sitting room that was the billiard room created by John Squire around 1900. This sitting room was used by the Sansom Whites for parties for friends and their families, such parties being more formal and structured than would be normal in the twenty-first century of today; entertainment was often offered in the shape of a conjuror or the like. In the sale brochure for the hotel in 1955 this room was described as a Residents' Lounge and was later to become the Bedford Bar.

Food was still rationed in 1944 and the living-in staff had an allowance of biscuits once a fortnight but there appeared to have been no major deprivations. All vegetables and flowers were grown in the hotel garden (now the Bedford Car Park). Chamberpots, plain white, were still provided in 1944 and were available in all rooms until 1955.

Margaret Mary White, known as Mary, married Royal Marine Capt Patrick John Ovens MC in Tavistock Parish Church on 24 April 1952, warranting front-page photograph(s) in the *Tavistock Gazette*. The wedding was large with 180 guests and, likely due to the hotel being physically unable to cater for so many guests, the reception venue was not the Bedford, but Tavistock Town Hall, followed by the honeymoon of the period – motor touring. The bride and groom, who had

Presentation of long service awards by the manager Geoffrey Stockman – c1970
L to R – William Yelland, Geoffrey Stockman, Sheila Stoneman, Samuel Chamings

David Gee – still going strong after 38 years service

won an MC in Korea, made their future home in Southsea. Mary White was deeply into Conservative Party politics of the day.

On Valentine's Day 1953 Anthony George White married Dawn Orynthia Bontoft in St Eustachius's Church, Tavistock. The reception was held at the Bedford and the happy couple, after a touring honeymoon, returned to Coventry where they had met and where Anthony worked in the Aviation Division of the Dunlop Rubber Company, having decided the hotel business was not for him. Anthony's brother-in-law, Capt Patrick John Ovens was one of the ushers and the parents, Sansom Whites, and grandfather, William Isaac Lake, also enjoyed the celebrations.

In 1948 William Lake extended his lease on the hotel for a further 7 years at £830pa later increased to £845. But difficult times were ahead. In 1948 also the hotel was 'invaded' by actors and film crew for the making of 'Escape', a movie about an escape from Dartmoor Prison starring Rex Harrison and Peggy Cummins, among others.

By the late 1940s the layout of the hotel at 'ground floor' level ie hotel entrance floor level, was different to today. The Ladies' rest room was where the Gents' is today and the bar area was a sitting room, one of two, the other being the present lounge area on the front of the hotel. Hotel Reception was smaller than today but in the same area and adjacent to this was a further Sitting Room. To the south of reception was a small office area, said to be c1920, which protruded over the inner courtyard. This addition was demolished to make way for the new Gallery 26 extension in 2009. After the 1920s little or no major change was undertaken which altered the hotel 'footprint' apart from the demolition of the old stable block across the stable yard, today's car park, which was demolished in the 1970s, and, post 1988, the removal of the garage buildings on the west side of the car park. Externally the hotel had changed little to the eye with the exception, perhaps, of a new painted sign on the eastern end wall, shown by Frith in 1934; today this has gone leaving a lighter patch on that wall. By the 1950s nothing had changed from the NW view with the exception of a peculiar 'shed' over the entrance porch, still visible today.

In 1939 Lake had described his terms as 'moderate' but how 'moderate' the tariff was is difficult to say, firstly, because all such things are relative to their time and, secondly, because little reliable contemporary documentary evidence is available up to the mid 1950s. Surviving evidence from directories and handbooks of the Michelin and the AA and RAC indicate the following prices for Bed and Breakfast in the hotel

1916 – 5/9 to 7/6	(28p to 38p)
1927 – 10/- to 13/6	(50p to 43p)
1933 – 10/6 to 14/-	(53p to 70p)
1955 – 21/- to 22/6	(£1.05 to £1.13)

Various contemporary bills for hotel services survive and add to and confirm specific information to that in the roadbooks.

The charges that any hotel makes for services etc likely reflects, in part, the wage bills for staff. Little has been found for such data for the Bedford with the exception of recollections of Douglas Roberts who was born in Tavistock in 1919. On leaving school Doug was offered a place as a

TELEGRAMS·
BEDFORD HOTEL
TAVISTOCK.

TELEPHONE Nº 37.

Tariff.

Bedford Hotel, Tavistock.

W. I. LAKE.
PROPRIETOR.

TAVISTOCK on the Main Coach Road between Plymouth and London is situated in the beautiful Valley of the Tavy, on the fringe of Dartmoor, and is recognised as one of the gates of the "Ancient Forest," is in close proximity to Princetown, Endsleigh (the beautiful cottage of the Duke of Bedford) Lydford Gorge and Waterfall, Morwell Rocks and the charmingly wooded slopes of the Tamar, and from here the most varied and delightful scenery in Devonshire can be easily and quickly visited.

THE BEDFORD HOTEL (part of the ancient abbey) is rep'ete with all modern requirements for the comfort and convenience of visitors, and is officially appointed by the **Royal Automobile Club** and the **Automobile Association.**

Three packs of hounds meet during the season within easy distance of the Hotel, and excellent **Salmon and Trout Fishing** can be obtained in the local streams, this being one of the features of the neighbourhood.

Extensive Stabling with nine large loose boxes for gentlemen's hunters, and lock-up coach houses.

Posting in all its branches.   Motor Garage, pit and petrol.

The Golf Links, 18 Holes, (within ten minutes walk of the Hotel) are among the finest and most natural Links in England.

Ball Room for public and private parties. Excellent **Billiard Room.**

Garden (2 acres) attached to Hotel for Visitors' use.

Hotel 'Bus meets principal L. &. S. W. Railway and G. W. Railway trains.

NO CHARGE IS MADE FOR ATTENDANCE.

❧ TARIFF. ❧

Apartments.		Luncheons.	
SINGLE BEDROOM ... per day, from **4/6**		BASIN OF SOUP **1/-**	
DOUBLE ,, ... ,, ,, **8/6**		HOT OR COLD, SWEETS AND CHEESE **2/6**	
DRESSING ROOM ... ,, ,, **2/-**			
PRIVATE SITTING ROOM ... ,, ,, **6/-**		Teas.	
		CUP OF TEA, COFFEE, OR COCOA... ... **6d.**	
Fires.		PLAIN TEA **1/-**	
		,, ,, WITH EGGS **1/6**	
SITTING ROOM ... ... per day, **1/6**		,, ,, ,, COLD MEAT ... **2/-**	
BEDROOM ... ... ,, **1/6**			
DO. ... ... after 5 p.m. **1/-**		Dinner.	
		DINNER TABLE D'HOTE **4/-**	
Baths.			
		Visitors' Servants.	
HIP OR SPONGE IN BEDROOM... ... **6d.**		BOARD, per day **5/-**	
HOT OR COLD IN BATH ROOM **1/-**		BEDROOM **2/-**	
Breakfasts.		*Boarding Terms from £3/3/- per week,*	
		or 10/6 per day, from October to June.	
PLAIN **1/6**		*Summer Terms on application.*	
COLD MEAT OR EGGS **2/-**			
HOT, One Course **2/6**		DOGS (kept in kennels) ... ... per day **1/-**	
,, Two Courses **3/-**			

Meals served in private rooms are charged **6d.** extra each person.

Tariff for the Bedford Hotel c 1916

Kelly's Directory advertisement for the Bedford Hotel 1939

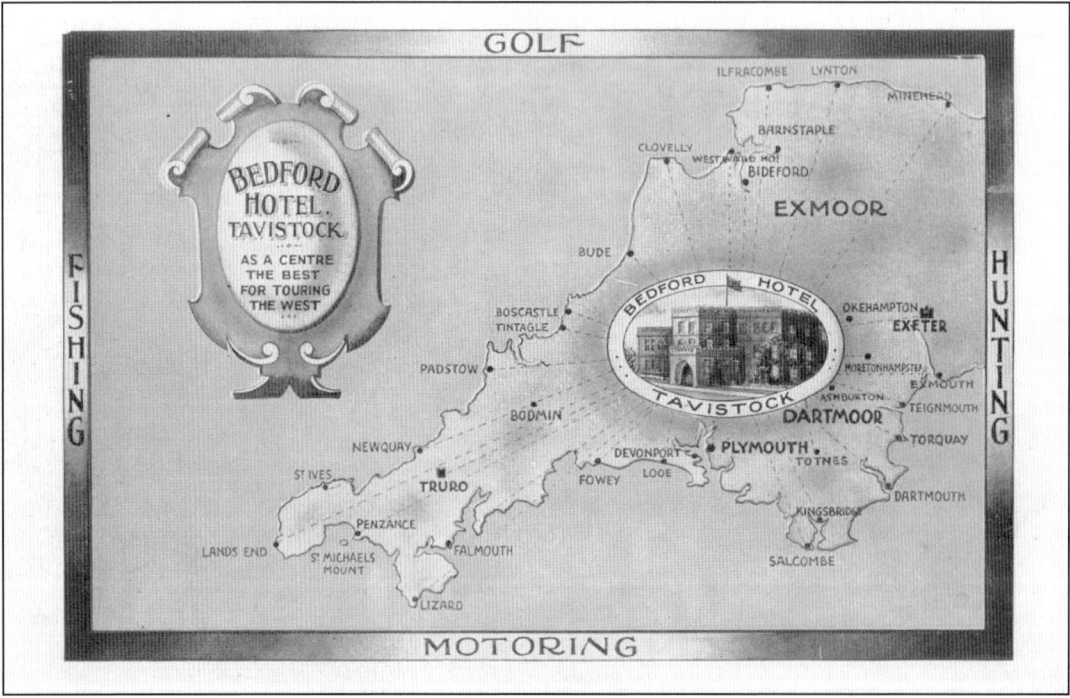

Advertising postcard for the Bedford hotel – 1950s

View from the north-east showing the painted sign on the north-east wall – c1934

View from the north-west showing addition above porch – postcard c1960?

trainee, or commis, chef at the Bedford. Remuneration package and contract was pay of sixpence a week, two and one half pence in today's bounty, for a period of five years, and on completion of that training Douglas would have been a fully trained chef – he did not take the job.

By 1927 the hotel was officially registered with both the AA and the RAC, an event that was exploited in advertising. The handbooks issued by these organisations also offer an insight into the number of available bedrooms, which were given as 25 in 1927 and 30 throughout the period 1933 to 1955. By 1939 Lake was advertising hot and cold in every bedroom. There would appear to have been no development works in this period although at some date before 1939 a curious looking shed-like structure appeared over the entrance lobby.

William Isaac Lake was a staunch Conservative and for a long period was a member of the Committee of the Tavistock Conservative Association. A keen athlete at the turn of the century he played back as an amateur for Plymouth Argyle whom he supported until his death. According to his granddaughter William had played soccer in the moat of the Tower of London during his early years in Romford. He was a devoted churchman and churchwarden at St Andrews, Plymouth, for twenty-three years. William retired through ill health in 1953 and lived out his days in the family home of Calumet in Western College Road in Plymouth where he died on Boxing Day 1958 at the age of 88: he was cremated after a private funeral service at St Andrews Church. William was survived by his second wife, Agnes. His business, the Bedford Hotel was, 3 years before his death, sold by the House of Bedford and was to become, for the next 50 years, a small cog in the wheels of big business.

By the end of William Lake's 'reign' in 1955 the view of the Bedford Hotel from the north east was little different to that enjoyed today; 187 years of looking at the same face in the mirror, no ageing, no deterioration, no lack of welcoming arms. However, the end of Lake's tenure was a temporary end to private ownership of this delightful and much loved hotel. Big business was on the prowl.

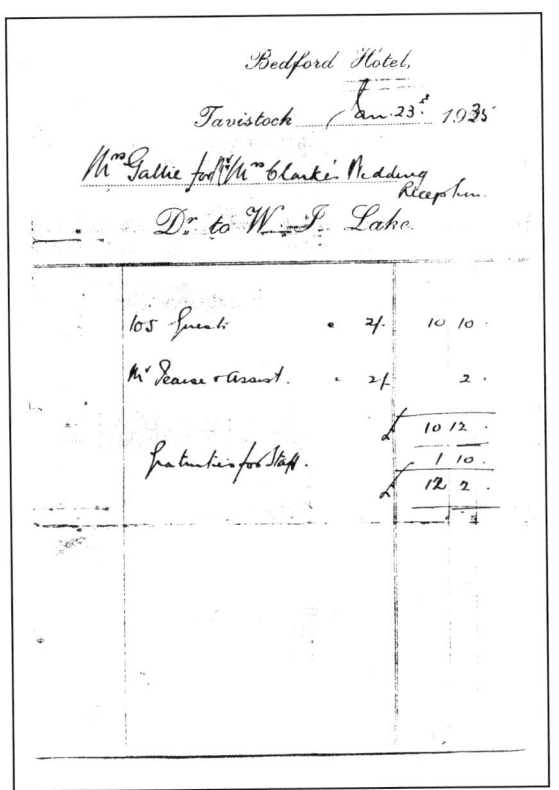

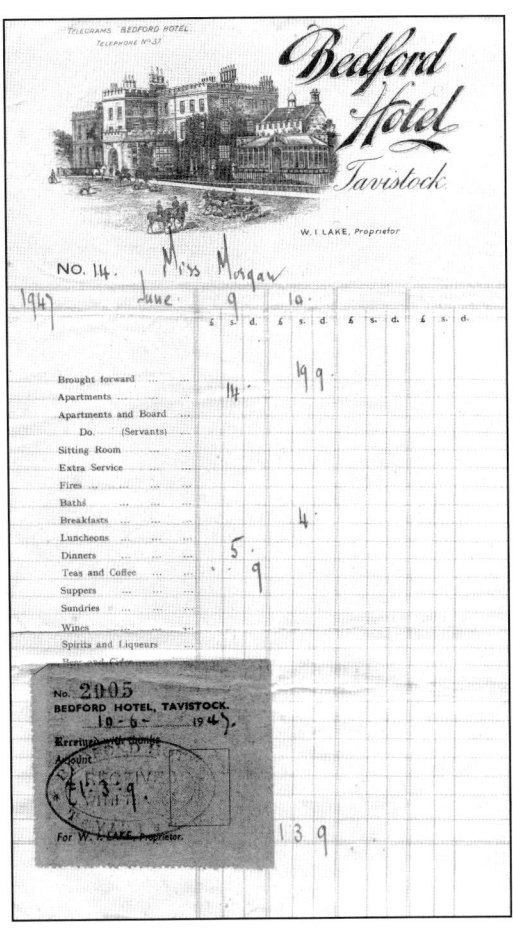

Bedford Hotel,

Tavistock   Jan 23ʳᵈ 1935

Mrs Gallie for Mr & Mrs Clarke Wedding
Reception.

Dr. to W. I. Lake.

105 Guests	2/.	10	10
Mr Pearse + Assist.	2/.	2	
	£	10	12
Gratuities for Staff.		1	10
	£	12	2

TELEGRAMS BEDFORD HOTEL
TELEPHONE Nº 37

Bedford Hotel
Tavistock.

W. I. LAKE, Proprietor.

NO. 114.   Miss Morgan

1947	June	9			10									
		£	s	d	£	s	d	£	s	d	£	s	d	
Brought forward						1	9	9						
Apartments		14												
Apartments and Board														
Do. (Servants)														
Sitting Room														
Extra Service														
Fires							4							
Baths														
Breakfasts														
Luncheons														
Dinners		5												
Teas and Coffee			9											
Suppers														
Sundries														
Wines														
Spirits and Liqueurs														

No. 2005
BEDFORD HOTEL, TAVISTOCK.
19 - 6 -   1947.
Received with thanks
Amount

For W. I. LAKE, Proprietor.   1 3 9

TRUSTHOUSE FORTE U.K. LIMITED
REMITTANCES TO

thf

Paid with Thanks
£1

SALE INVOICE   Date 13 March 1987

BREAKFASTS	
LUNCHEONS	
AFTERNOON-TEAS	
DINNERS	25 00
HORS D'OEUVRE, SOUPS, OM'TES etc	
FISH	
ENTREES ROAST, GRILLS COLD BUFFET	
VEGETABLES and SALADS	
SWEETS, CHEESE and SAVOURIES	
COFFEE	
BEERS & MINERALS	
WINES	£7 75
SPIRITS & LIQUEURS	
CIGARS & CIGARETTES	
INVOICE TOTAL INCLUDING % VAT, *	£40 50

Reg. Office 12 Sherwood Street, London W1V 7RD

COVERS 2	CATERING SERVICES EXCL. V.A.T.	
	V.A.T. %	
TABLE No. 19	* INVOICE TOTAL INCL. %V.A.T.	

ROOM No.   NAME

ADDRESS

V.A.T. REGISTRATION No. 232 2014 27
PRICES INCLUDE SERVICE and V.A.T.   AM 000331

Bills from the Bedford Hotel for 1935, 1947 and 1987

The End of the Bedford Family Influence

In October 1953 the twelfth Duke of Bedford, Hastings William Sackville Russell, was found shot in the head in bushes in the grounds of Endsleigh, the Bedford family's cottage near Milton Abbot. The circumstances of his death are described by his son John, who was to succeed to the title as the 13th Duke of Bedford. John writes

"Apparently my father had gone out about seven o'clock in the morning on Friday, 9 October with his gun to shoot hawks or cormorants, as was his usual practice. When he did not return for lunch, the estate people started looking for him, and by the following morning a full-scale search had been organised … They were on the point of dragging the river Tamar when his body was found by two estate workers in some undergrowth off a small private drive not five hundred yards from the house. He had died instantaneously from a gunshot wound in the head.

The verdict was accidental death. Like so many of his ancestors, my father's sight had been failing for some time, and it may be that he stumbled, although what an experienced shot could have been doing going round through undergrowth with his gun cocked and loaded instead of broken is, I must confess, beyond me. There are certainly those who think it was not an accident …"

After over 400 years of 'collecting' property the Bedford Estate was valued at £8 million and the taxman was waiting to pounce and collect his share, a reasonable £4.5 million, in death duties. The result was almost inevitable, some of the properties had to be sold and Tavistock was finally to sever its last direct links with the Bedford family. In November 1954 the Bedford Estate gave William Lake notice and eventually an agreement was reached whereby Lake received a payment of £1250 for the surrender of his rights and was allowed to have the property rent-free until the end of October 1955 – a good deal for Lake considering his lease was due to run out in March 1955.

On 18 March 1955 the *Tavistock Gazette* announced that negotiations were in progress between the Tavistock Urban District Council and the Bedford Estate for the purchase of the Bedford Hotel kitchen garden, described as 'a delightful old-world garden'. Two months later the lead article proclaimed

"So now it is out that Tavistock Urban Council have purchased the Bedford Hotel Garden and intend converting it into a car park.

… All will be sorry that the gardens have to be destroyed. We hope that at least

Hastings William Sackville Russell (1888-1953), 12th Duke of Bedford – copyright National Portrait Gallery

some of the borders along the walls and some of the trees will be preserved, where at all possible.

Laid out with imagination, a car park need not be the dreary tarmac area many of them are ..."

For some 40 years the hotel garden had been lovingly tended single-handed by Charlie Doidge who lived at 38 Brook Street in Tavistock. Charlie had left school at twelve to become a pageboy at Kelly House. Preferring outdoor work he then became a gardener/coachman at Kelly 'for half a crown a week and my keep' and met his future wife, Dorothy Anne Rogers, the cook at Endsleigh, whom he married in the autumn of 1897. By 1901 Charlie and Dorothy lived at 16 Exeter Street, Tavistock, and worked for a short time for the Freeman family at Abbotsfield, Tavistock, and then on to the Bedford Hotel around 1904.

Trevor James, Charlie's grandson, described the garden and Charlie's involvement thus

"He grew everything. I recall seeing potatoes, all kinds of green vegetables, carrots, beetroots, lettuces, and of course tomatoes and cucumbers, in the big greenhouse in the middle of the garden which had a boiler underneath and a large iron water tank on the outside. All the water was taken from the Tavistock Canal, which flowed along one side as it still does. The garden was divided into squares where the products were grown with box hedging all round and neatly trimmed at all times to a height of about 2ft. Besides the vegetables there were every kind of fruit, from raspberries and gooseberries to red and black currants, strawberries, apples and pears. On either side of the path which runs from the Plymouth Road entrance to the little bridge that spans the canal, there were apple and pear trees growing on the walls and polyanthus at their foot all the way along. Weeds were not allowed.

My grandfather had no mechanical aids which meant the entire garden was dug by hand – how he did it I will never know but he worked until he was seventy years of age ... I don't think he earned more than £3 a week in his life but never was there a more conscientious employee .... A gentleman called White owned the hotel at that time and as a mark of appreciation for services faithfully rendered he gave his gardener £1 per week out of his own pocket when he retired. Not long afterwards Mr White died and my grandfather lost his £1 a week ... "

Charlie was particularly fond of growing flowers and became a noted judge at the local flower shows in the area. He was a Committee member of the Tavistock Cottage Garden Society, a member of the British Legion, the Royal and Ancient Order of the Buffaloes and of the Independent Order of Oddfellows with an added post as a Trustee of the Abbey Chapel.

When Charlie Doidge retired, aged 70, his place as gardener of the Bedford was taken for a short time by a gentleman named Hoare followed by Edward Walters who had first worked as gardener at Tavistock Vicarage, next door to the Bedford garden. Edward and Harry had chatted through the hole in the wall between the two gardens and on hearing of Charlie's imminent retirement Edward applied for, and got, the job as gardener at the hotel.

Charlie Doidge, Hotel gardener 1904 to 1947, with Trevor James and friend Joyce Box

Charlie Doidge lived out his days at Browne's Memorial Cottages in Tavistock where he and his wife had lived since June 1945. He died on 19 April 1959 aged 82 and his wife, Dorothy Anne lived on to the magnificent age of 97. She died on 20 February 1970 and lies reunited with Charlie in Plymouth Road Cemetery.

Whilst the hotel garden proper was used to supply fresh produce to the hotel use was made of the hotel grounds for other worthy purposes and for a short period after World War 2 the Dolvin Road School had a patch of ground in the small hotel garden adjacent to the Still Tower for gardening classes under a teacher called Mr Shaw.

A correspondent to the *Tavistock Gazette* at the time of the sale in 1955 voiced disapproval of the car park proposal and had the temerity to suggest that some on the council "might even put merry-go-rounds there!". Subsequently this tranquil corner of the town, purchased by the Council for the princely sum of £700, was to be covered in lifeless tar macadam as a car park, no borders, no trees, no imagination, no sensitive town planning – nothing changes. The correspondent was, however, not to be disappointed because years later, at every Goose Fair, the merry-go-rounds and fair stalls are welcomed in the car park.

Subsequently there was talk in high places about improving the access to the car park because there was a reticence to use this facility, a reticence not caused by high charges because it was free parking (perhaps some things do change), but more because the residents of Tavistock and visitors considered it to be a God given right to park anywhere in town – no, nothing changes.

Soon the one time narrow pathway alongside the vicarage garden was widened to allow an alternative vehicle access to the car park but, as far as is known, was never used as such and in 2012 is solely for pedestrians.

In June of 1955 the Bedford Estate gave the Tavistock UDC the freehold of the Still House and in September it was announced that the Bedford Hotel was to be sold along with much more of the Bedford Estate in Devon. The *Tavistock Gazette* of 10 June noted that

> "Early in this century a new lounge was added and the hotel ballroom converted to two floors of bedrooms.
>
> For the past 30 years it has been managed by Mr and Mrs R J Sansom White ... the lease held by Mr W I Lake."

The conversion of the ballroom to bedrooms was likely between 1930, when the hotel was the venue for Tavistock Badminton Club, and 1933 when the number of bedrooms had increased to the 30 noted in the AA Handbook from the 25 noted in the 1927; the badminton club had relocated to the Town Hall by January 1933.

September 1955 was the real turning point in the life of the Bedford Hotel for on the fifteenth day of that month the Bedford Hotel came under the hammer of Humbert and Flint, of London, in conjunction with Clutton and Drew of Tavistock, with possession on completion on 2 January 1956. The sale catalogue is of interest in its provision of, among others, details of the

Foulston's 1830's Bedford Hotel ballroom pictured in 2012. The three pairs of double windows were originally three full length windows lighting the large ballroom inside, now showing the new floor introduced to offer extra bedrooms in the 1930s. The last remains of the original stables are shown on the right

internal arrangement at that date. It also claims the building was built about 1720 "by the Third Duke of Bedford in a castellated style ... ", the reference to the Third Duke is incorrect – in true estate agent tradition.

The Sale Catalogue describes the hotel facilities thus

ON THE GROUND FLOOR

Entrance hall – 19ft 6in by 13ft 3in
Reception Office and Manager's Office
Dining Room – panelled and L-shaped 32ft 6in by 18 ft and 11ft 6in by 14ft with fireplace and central heating. There is a small room adjoining containing sinks, cupboards etc and the lift to the kitchen
Residents' Lounge – 26ft 3in by 18ft 3in with fireplace and central heating
Sun veranda – (off the Residents' Lounge) 33ft 3in by 9ft with Service Room off
Three Sitting Rooms – 17ft 3in by 16ft 3in; 17ft 9in by 15ft and 18ft by 16ft 9in respectively, all with fireplaces
Smoke Room – 15ft 9in by 8ft 3in with fireplace
Cocktail Bar – 17ft by 11ft 6in with fireplace
Lounge Hall – 26ft by 16ft 6in with central heating
Lounge – 21ft by 18ft with fireplace
Five bedrooms – Four double, one single; all with lavatory basins

Gentlemen's Toilet containing two lavatory basins and other sanitary fittings
Ladies' Toilet containing three WCs and two lavatory basins
WC and Boot Room

ON THE LOWER GROUND FLOOR

Tap Bar – 13ft 9in by 9ft 3in with fireplace
Public Sitting Room – 20ft 6in by 12ft with fireplace
Private Sitting Room – 13ft 3in by 11ft 9in with fireplace
Kitchen – 32ft by 20ft 6in with coal fired range, gas cooker, potato peeler etc and service lift to dining room
Staff Hall, Two Bedrooms, Changing Room

Scullery – Two Larders, Grocery Store, Dairy, Knife Room, Linen Room, WC
Boiler House – with Britannia Beeston Boilers, Coal House, Wood Store and Four Cellars

ON THE FIRST FLOOR

Fourteen Bedrooms – Seven Single and seven double, all with lavatory basins and eleven with fireplaces
Two Bathrooms
Staff Wing – containing six bedrooms, Bathroom with lavatory basin and WC
Ladies' Toilet containing two WCs and one lavatory basin

Gentlemen's Toilet (on half-landing) containing two WCs and two lavatory basins
Service Room with lavatory basin and sluice

ON THE SECOND FLOOR

Ten Bedrooms – Four Double and Six Single all with lavatory basins and nine with fireplaces
Bathroom – containing bath and lavatory basin

Linen Room and two WCs

SUMMARY OF PRINCIPAL ACCOMMODATION

Dining Room	Twenty-nine Guest Bedrooms	Three Principal Lounges
Five Bathrooms	Two Bars Staff Accommodation	Smoke Room
Domestic Offices	Manager's Accommodation	Garages for 26 cars

SERVICES

Main Water – with Beeston and Britannia Boilers serving the domestic hot water and central heating system respectively
Main Electric Light and Power
Gas and **Drainage** to Public Sewer

OUTSIDE

THE GARAGES for twenty-six cars stand around a large yard. The lower yard contains a workshop and a range of stabling. The workshop and that part of the yard now in use will remain in the occupation of the vendors until 31st March 1956. See Special Conditions for rights of enjoyed by Tavistock UDC.

THE GARDEN extends to about 27 perches and is situated between the canal and the River Tavy. It is bounded on the south side by part of the ancient Tavistock Abbey Wall. See Special Conditions for rights of enjoyed by Tavistock UDC.

The garden is let to the Rev B J Guy on an annual Lady Day tenancy at a rent of 10s per annum

Outgoings – Total Rateable value £537; NAV Income tax Schedule "A" £446 10s 0d

WITH VACANT POSSESSION at 1st November 1955 (except for the lower garden and lower yard)

Also offered for sale on the same day, but separately to the hotel, were the Fishing Rights including the freehold of half the river bed in part of the River Tavy, from Carrion Pool in the north to the footbridge to Lady Bertha Mine in the south, a distance of some 4 miles. The Tavy

Humbert and Flint Sale catalogue for the Bedford Hotel, September 1955

On Instruction from W. I. LAKE, Esq.

THE BEDFORD HOTEL, TAVISTOCK.

SALE TUESDAY NEXT 25th OCTOBER 1955, at 11 a.m.

AND

TWO FOLLOWING DAYS

WARD and CHOWEN

Will Sell by Auction on the Premises, commencing each day at **11 a.m.**, the whole of the contents of the Bedford Hotel, comprising:

THE FURNISHINGS

OF

30 BEDROOMS

LOUNGES, DINING ROOM

SITTING ROOMS

AND

BAR and SMOKE ROOM FURNITURE

Large Quantity of **TABLE PLATE, CHINA and GLASS**
Table and Bed Linen,
Collection of **Old Prints and Pictures.**
EXCELLENT CARPETS.

Full particulars in Catalogues Price 1/- obtainable at the offices of the Auctioneers from Thursday, 20th October.

Admission to **VIEWING** and **SALE** by **CATALOGUE ONLY.**

ON VIEW: Monday, 24th October, 1955, at 11 a.m. to 5 p.m.

ORDER OF SALE:

Tuesday, 25th—Bedroom Furniture.

Wednesday, 26th—Lounge and other Furniture.

Thursday, 27th—Plate, Table and Bed Linen, etc.

Auction Offices, 1, Church Lane, Tavistock.
Telephone: Tavistock 41 and 458.

Advertisement for sale of hotel effects in October 1955

at that time had a reputation for salmon, peal and trout fishing and contained some noted salmon pools.

The sale period itself was to be very quiet for the hotel staff – they all took their holidays. The mood in other circles was not so tranquil.

The Tavistock Rural District Council of the day had visions of grandeur and had earmarked some £20000 (some £350000 in today's money) in their budget for the purchase and development of the Bedford Hotel to offices for their own use; at the time they occupied offices in the lately redundant Temperance Hotel in Pym Street, now the Ordulph Arms public house. However, the Urban District Council were most upset that they had not been consulted especially as the move, if completed, would increase the local Council Rates. Two days before the sale the UDC took evasive action by threatening to refuse planning permission for the conversion, a move that they did not, in practice, totally control. Amidst cries of 'rotter', 'cad', 'unfair' etc the childish bantering carried on for some two months, before the peace pipes were eventually passed around.

Prior to auction day other interested parties were also drawing up plans for purchase of the property; these included the National Coal Board and a syndicate of Tavistock townspeople. However, on auction day, 15 September 1955, the auction was a damp squib, despite the bidding being opened by the RDC. From an opening bid of £12000, bidding stopped at £17350 and the property was withdrawn to be sold by private treaty on 19 September, to the hotel chain Trust Houses Ltd for £17750. The fishing rights were sold for £3200 to Lt Col G C Cross, a local bank manager and on 25 to 27 October the entire contents of the Bedford Hotel, the property of William Isaac Lake, came under the hammer wielded by Ward and Chowen of Tavistock.

Trust Houses reopened the hotel on 1 November 1955, the first managers being Mr and Mrs B J Dodridge, natives of Plymouth, who had previous assistant managerial experience at the Dartmoor Inn at Merrivale, followed by full managership of the Lansdowne Arms at Calne in Wiltshire. Within a few months refurbishment of the Veranda Bar was completed by J Kerswill and Son, builders of Tavistock. The fireplace was of rusticated slate from Longford Quarry, supplied by Stedman's of Tavistock, as was the crazy paving laid at the entrance – thus keeping up a tradition of the use of local tradesmen.

The long serving Sansom Whites moved to the Blue Lion in Lewdown but both continued to hold local office in Tavistock, Mrs Sansom White, as an Officer of the Red Cross and past President of the Townswomen's Guild, and her husband as the Chairman of the local newspaper, the *Tavistock Gazette*. They lived out their final days in Exeter. Throughout their residency at the Bedford the Sansom Whites were referred to by that name, rather than the correct simple name of White under which all matters legal, such as births, marriages and deaths, appear to have been recorded. It would be argued by some that the status of the Bedford Hotel warranted a double-barrelled surname.

William Isaac Lake died in Plymouth aged 88 on Boxing Day 1958 by which time the Trust House management had got well into the running of the Bedford Hotel.

Trust Houses started in their tradition of running hotels where you would take your 'best girl' when you wished to impress, or plead forgiveness. The Bedford was an hotel where the guests went to functions and looked forward to the 'dressing up'. It was an hotel which did its level best to please its customers and the hotel went out of its way to ensure that, for example, a wedding breakfast at the hotel was, in itself, an occasion. Leslie Miles and Marion Hartley, now Miles, were to remember for the rest of their lives that special day. Leslie writes

"We were married on Saturday 4th August 1956 (Bank Holiday) at St. Eustachius Church. As we left the church after the service we were showered with confetti by children from the primary school, where Marion was a teacher. Photographs were taken in the churchyard with the Town Hall as a backdrop. We walked across the road to the reception in the Bedford Hotel, a kindly policeman holding up the traffic.

.... the photo of us cutting the cake ... is memorable as the cake was made by the hotel chef ... Chammings (we think that is the correct name) and given to us by the Bedford. Marion's father, Cyril Hartley, French master and deputy head at Tavistock Grammar school, taught Mr. Chammings, and Marion taught his son."

The chef was Samuel Chamings and his son was Bernard.

Mr and Mrs Miles cutting the Chamings's wedding cake – 4 August 1956

In October 1962, the lease to the porch to the Abbey Chapel ie the Bedford Dairy, was handed to G G Pearse Esq, Chairman of the Tavistock UDC. The terms were a 99-year lease on the property at an annual rental of one peppercorn. In order that the Council did not run out of funds Trust Houses additionally gave a bag of peppercorns with the lease. This medieval porch had accessed the Abbot's Lodging (the present day Abbey Chapel) and Mrs Bray in 1879 describes the porch thus

> "At the back of the Abbey House (now the Bedford Hotel) stands a porch, crowned with four lofty pinnacles, partially covered with the most luxuriant ivy. The ceiling of the vaulted entrance is of elegantly carved stonework. The upper room is also vaulted with pendant woodwork. In it is a chimney. As there was no communication to it, the doorway in a different direction being blocked up, a passage was broken through the wall a few years since, near one of the corners, where there is a hollow buttress or turret ... The porch here described leads to what was supposed to be the Abbot's Hall."

Whilst the ceiling of the lower floor remains intact today all trace of the upper room features have long since been removed.

Access to the Abbey Chapel previous to c1845 was via the southern entrance to the Abbey Porch which was subsequently blocked off around 1845 when the frame of the old water-gate of the abbey buildings along the river bank was inserted into the east wall of the Chapel. A drawing of the dairy in 1866 by E Appleton shows the layout of the benching within the archway upon which the dairy goods were stored and worked. The Abbey Chapel Porch, was known in its later years as the Bedford Dairy and Rachel Evans in her earlier work on Tavistock

The Dairy, Bedford Hotel, Tavistock – engraving by Rock & Co, 1846

Abbey Chapel porch alias the Old Dairy – 1910

Part of a drawing of the Bedford Dairy by E Appleton in 1866 showing the Bedford Dairy benching

in 1846 had written

> "The archway is now used as a dairy in which is deposited the rich clouted cream and delicious milk, made of service in providing entertainment for his guests by mine host of the Hotel."

It is likely that around this time the entrance to the Chapel via the archway in its southern wall was blocked off to form the Bedford Dairy. The dairy benching has long since disappeared and some time after 1962 the northern entrance to the porch was also blocked off and a side access made from the grounds of the Abbey Chapel. Whilst accesses have been blocked off and opened up the magnificent granite vaulted ceiling of the porch, with its Caen stone bosses, remain, likely viewing such goings on with haughty indifference and disdain. This ceiling remains in fine fettle in 2012.

In its turn the Trust House organisation also made its mark on the fabric of the hotel. At acquisition the hotel comprised 29 guest bedrooms, all with hot and cold; 4 guest bathrooms; ladies' and gentlemen's toilets; plus 8 staff bedrooms with one bathroom. With various changes within the hotel the number of bedrooms gradually reduced from 29 at sale in 1955 through to 26 in 1970/71 and at Easter 1971 the hotel boasted 26 bedrooms, six with en-suite bathroom facilities. The major changes were to come after 1970 when the Trust Houses Group merged with Forte Holdings Ltd to form Trust House Forte (THF). In that year the then resident manager Mr Stockman suggested that the staff bedrooms be converted into guest bedrooms and the staff housed locally away from the hotel at No 3 Vigo Bridge Road in Tavistock, Stockman himself continuing to live in-house. Under the in-house direction of Geoffrey Stockman, the demands of the modern traveller resulted in a major £45000 facelift to give

> "... a new Cocktail Bar by Christmas, which is being built in part of the residents' lounge just off reception.

> The rest of the work includes a complete refurbishment of all the bedrooms, new kitchens, five new private bathrooms and two more bedrooms ... The hotel gardens are also being overhauled ... An enlarged car park has recently been built behind the hotel."

The changes gave a hotel with 33 bedrooms, 17 with en-suite facilities and the stable block appears to have been demolished, possibly in two stages, for the above mentioned car park facility. Other alterations were to follow; the Tap bar was to be closed to the public in 1976 and the comfortable Bedford Bar was converted from the residents' lounge, ie the billiard room provided by John Squire, and the veranda which had been added in Lake's tenancy. In 1977 the Bedford Bar was 'reopened' by the then Tavistock Mayor, John Philpott. Also by 1976/7 a further 4 bedrooms had been added giving an advertised total of 37 rooms. It is likely that access to the veranda was opened up at this stage directly from the old billiard room.

The new Bedford Bar was to prove very popular as a place to meet, especially amongst established residents of the town and the up and coming middle class set. In the late 1970s the bar was to play an important part in the ritualistic rehearsals of the local thespians who would meet here every night prior to final rehearsals in the Town Hall, and likely afterwards.

At some time during this period also a major change was to take place in the main restaurant. A fixed wall at the western end was replaced with a mobile, folding door system which allowed the restaurant to be left open or divided into two rooms. The photograph below shows both the fixed wall and the style of hotel furnishings of the period.

On taking over the hotel in 1955 Trust houses appeared to offer rates below the last year of Lake's tenure but slowly, as sure as dawn comes tomorrow, the prices for B and B increased

1955 – 18/6 to 21/-	(£0.93 to £1.05)
1959 – 23/6 to 25/-	(£1.18 to £1.25)
1964 – 27/6 to 37/6	(£1.38 to £1.88)
1966 – 30/- to 40/-	(£1.50 to £2.00)
1971 – 42/-	(£2.10) – bed only
1988 – £25	

As surely also, was the annual Goose Fair Day, an event celebrated for many years in the hostelries in Tavistock by almost all except the geese, and the Boxing Day Hunt meeting at the Bedford Hotel, enjoyed by on-lookers but considered with some apprehension by all but very confident foxes.

Various advertising material is extant for the Bedford during the THF period some of it not only showing the food on offer but also the tariff prices.

Reference has been made above to long-serving staff members of the Bedford Hotel but this brief history would not be complete without brief mention of at least two long term residents, although there were very likely more than just two examples. The first was Henry Davey. Born in Lewtrenchard in 1843 Henry was educated Tavistock Grammar School in Russell Street followed by training in Nicholl's and Matthews's iron foundry, the Bedford Iron Works, in Lakeside. Eventually Henry moved to Leeds where he co-founded the engineering firm of Hathorne, Davey and Company where he became an acknowledged expert in the field of hydraulic machinery, a member of the Institute of Civil Engineers and technical author. In 1908 Henry Davey retired to Tavistock and for five years lived at the Bedford Hotel before moving to Woburn Terrace where he died in 1928. He counted former Prime Minister Ramsey Macdonald amongst his friends and Macdonald visited him in Tavistock only to arrive on the day of Henry's funeral which took place in Plymouth Road Cemetery.

The second known long-term resident was Capt. Cecil Frank Hunter, who instead of just booking in for a weekend break, lived as a hotel guest from at least 1964 until moving into a nursing home in 1995. Capt. Hunter occupied room 24 for the whole of this time as it was, in 1964, the only room with en-suite facilities. Born in 1899 in Northfleet Cecil Hunter served a cadetship in sailing ships in WW1 and his career in the Merchant Navy involved cable laying and repair of sub-marine cables, a profession followed by his father before him. Cecil moved to Tavistock, and the Bedford Hotel, on his retirement, to be near his sister Myra Emanuel who lived at Bedford

Vaulted ceiling of the Abbey Porch in 2012. The original entrance from the Bedford Yard is on the right and access to the Abbey Chapel is on the left, both now blocked off

Restaurant pre-1983 showing the fixed wall at the west end (left) which was later replaced with a folding door

Remains of the stable block pictured in 1970. The whole block soon to be removed to enlarge the car park.

Official opening of the new Bedford Bar in 1977 by John Philpott, Mayor of West Devon.
L to R – Eddie Loendawhl, Hotel Manager; John Philpott; Mrs Philpott; Robin Start, Mayor of Tavistock;
Unknown; Mrs Martin; Bill Martin, Tavistock Town Clerk

Goose Fair advert in the Tavistock Gazette 1978

Brian Wills, Bedford Hotel chef, making sure the goose's goose is really cooked – Goose Fair Day 1979

Spooner's Hunt Boxing Day Meet outside the Bedford Hotel in 1978

James Lever, manager of the Bedford Hotel, offering the Stirrup Cup to the Spooner's Hunt
on Boxing Day 1987

House at Magpie Bridge, and near to his father who lived in Plymouth. Cecil died in Tavistock in 1996.

The year 1983 saw a major event in Tavistock in the visit of Prince Charles and Princess Diana, an event in which the Bedford Hotel was to play a large part offering rest room facilities to the Royals and 'the mouthwatering buffet for the official lunch' presented in the Town Hall by the Bedford Hotel chefs. It was Willie Stephens, the Second Chef, who actually served the Princess, who asked about the composition of some of the dishes. Perhaps the buffet was simply a larger version of the 'standard' Bedford Hotel buffet offered in the 1980s – for £3.50. A visit of royalty to an hotel was, indeed, a rare event and never to stay but just to use the 'facilities'. Such was the case at the visit of Charles and Diana but the management almost made a great faux-pas in allocating a room at front of house to the royal couple, thus possibly jeopardising the safety of the royal couple. Rob Sullivan, relieved that the event was just before his time, gives details

"Just before my time but I was told that a room had been refurbished for their use, 21 or 23 I think, as was the reception, lounge, stair well and bedroom corridor (the route they would take through the hotel). But when checked by the palace advanced guard, the hotel was informed front road facing rooms were not allowed so a single bedroom opposite on the corridor was hurriedly made good and decorated. I am led to believe the paint was only just dry when they used the facility …"

Visit of Prince Charles and Princess Diana to Tavistock in 1983. The Bedford Hotel is near at hand (top left) for that 'oh so welcome' comfort stop

Bedford Hotel

Introducing our new look luncheon
"BUFFET STYLE"
from Tuesday 5th. August

A full Buffet will be available at lunch times on Tuesday, Wednesday, Thursday and Saturday every week, with a fantastic selection of food to cater for all your tastes.

The various delights on our table will be exactly what you are seeking for a lunch time meal, and there really is a wide choice.

Starters
Home made soup
Brian's Chicken Liver Pâté
Terrine of Fish
Cornets of Ham and Prawns
Honeydew Melon with Port

Main Courses Cold
Roast Topside of Beef
Ham carved from the bone
Whole Roast Poussin
Fresh "Tavy" Trout
Quiche Lorraine

A wide and interesting selection of freshly made salads are always available to accompany your choice.

Main Courses Hot
The hot main course will change daily and these are some of the dishes you can expect to find.

Chicken Chasseur
Entrecote Bordalaise
Beef Bourguignonne
Hungarian Goulash
Veal Provençale

The choice of vegetables and/or salad are served with the hot dish.

Sweets
Cheese, Cheddar or Stilton

Cheesecake
Black Forest Gâteau
Fresh Fruit Salad
Chef's Apple Pie with Clotted Cream
Lemon Meringue Pie

So make a date for Lunch at the Bedford for only £3.50.   Tel: 3221
Service and V.A.T. inclusive.

Advertisement for the Bedford Hotel buffet lunches – September 1980

The buffet prepared in the Town Hall by the Bedford Hotel for the official Royal lunch.
L to R – Andrew Chamings, commis chef; Richard Crouch, commis chef;
Willie Stephens, Second Chef; Brian Wills, Head Chef

The royal car outside the Bedford Hotel awaiting the departure of
Prince Charles and Princess Diana

On Boxing Day 1983 the hotel was to suffer a major fire that damaged 12 bedrooms, staff accommodation and a garage containing two cars in the old ballroom area of the hotel and required the close attention of some 50 firemen. A pretty poor welcome for the new manager. Some 35 years later Rob Sullivan recalled his memory of the event

"The Bedford fire – I remember it well. I had only been at the Bedford a month. The night before we had held a UN charity function in the Russell Room ... We lit the fire in the fire place to make a hospitable evening venue. What we didn't know was there must have been a crack in the hearth (below was a void area where the staff assistant managers were parked). The coal fire was put out at the end of the evening. I was awoken at 7am on the Sunday morning with the fire bells. I ran down to reception and smelt burning, pushed open the Russell Room door and I saw the carpet seams smoking. In that micro second the smoke turned to fire like someone striking a match down the carpet. Needless to say the hotel was evacuated. The fire panel definitely saved lives that day.

I suppose the most emotional part for me was the sight of the Sunday morning with the road closed off, fire tenders and hoses and smoke being vented out of the front

Mandy Tugwell (nee Chamings) receives her tickets for her USA trip as winner of the Trust House Forte Receptionist of the Year Award 1983

doors and porch of the hotel. To add to this flames and smoke showing above and behind the Bedford Bar where the assistant managers' cars were burning …"

It is strange that adversity can sometimes lead to opportunity and it was the fire at the Bedford on Sunday 2 December 1983 that played a pivotal role in the selection, by Trust House Forte, of Mandy Tugwell, a receptionist at the Bedford Hotel, as 'The Receptionist of the Year Award 1983'. The 'Safety and Fire News' of February 1984 reported Mandy's win.

"Hotel receptionist Mandy Tugwell was quick to hand out breakfasts to tired and hungry firemen after a massive blaze at her hotel – but little did she think that it would help her win a £2000 trip to America.

For Mandy went on to compete for the title of receptionist of the year and her efforts were rewarded when she beat 11 other finalists and won the USA trip.

Although Mandy does not live in the Bedford Hotel, Tavistock, she was soon on the scene and helped restaurant staff serve food to some of the 50 firemen who fought the blaze.

By the way, Mandy's father is Tavistock Fire Chief Bernard Chamings who helped direct fire fighting at the hotel."

Andrew Chamings receives his Apprentice Chef Presentation from Rocco Forte in October 1985

The Chamings's connection with the Bedford Hotel was not isolated to Mandy and Bernard. Some 30 years previously Mandy's great-uncle, Samuel Chamings, had been the chef at the Bedford. On 22nd of October 1985 Mandy's brother, Andrew, a teenage chef at the Bedford Hotel, was presented by Rocco Forte with a set of chef's knives and a certificate at the Trust House Apprentice Chef Presentation at the Cumberland Hotel in London. Andrew continued his career as a chef and in 2012 is the head chef of a top restaurant in Tavistock. The Chamings's legacy continued when Chrissie Tugwell, Mandy's daughter, worked in the hotel in 2011.

In January 1985 THF spent some £60000 re-roofing the majority of the hotel and re-building thirteen chimneys. The work, which was necessitated because of leaks experienced over 'several years', was undertaken by Messrs Tuxfords of Wales – no undertaking here to use local professionals. The then manager, Mr Rob Sullivan gave assurance that similar materials were to be used and that the character of the chimneys would not be altered – possibly with the exception that they would not leak.

In September 1985 also the Bedford Bar, opened with great ceremony only eight years earlier,

Bedford Bar

at

The Bedford

HOTEL, TAVISTOCK

We are pleased to announce that following major refurbishment, the

Bedford Bar

has now Reopened

Opening at 5.30pm most evenings, we will be offering an initial

HAPPY HOUR

on Spirits and a Special Promotion on Carlsberg Lager

We look forward to welcoming you back 'in style' to the Bedford

Yours faiully

Press advertisement of 30 August 1985 announcing the Bedford Bar refurbishment

was completely refurbished by interior designer Bill Faux of Decorex Ltd of Dousland. The Tavistock Times described the works thus

> "The bar has a refurbished canopy, a bar rail for the feet and the blessing of Tavistock Town Mayor, Coun Dick Toop who said:
>
> 'One of the pleasant duties of being mayor is to walk into places in which you are made to feel at home. I do feel that here.'
>
> The manager, Mr Robert Sullivan, said that he owed much to the decorators and to Ushers, who had provided new dispensing equipment."

Despite the Ushers connection with the refurbishment the hotel was, and remains, a Free House.

These changes under manager Rob Sullivan were part of a programme of a very dynamic and innovative hotel manager who formed around himself a very enthusiastic team who enjoyed coming in to work every day. Special weekend events and singular evenings that were devoted to different cuisines were extremely successful. The then named Woburn Restaurant served locally sourced produce with local labels in the menu eg Chicken William Lake; roast beef

Visit of the Marquess of Tavistock to the Bedford Hotel in 1985.
L to R – Cllr Robin Fenner, Rob Sullivan, Marquess of Tavistock,
'Emsie' Toop, Mayor's Consort, Cllr Dick Toop, Tavistock Mayor

Tavistock Abbey; glazed leg of lamb Horndon; whole plaice Plymouth Sound; scallops on a skewer Duke of Bedford's Sword; Three Fillets Huckworthy, fillets of beef, veal and lamb – all served up in the romantic Woburn Restaurant. These days would also eagerly be welcomed back for the prices of £7.95 for a three-course lunch and £9.95 for a three-course dinner.

In 1985 it was Rob Sullivan's privilege to enjoy a very rare visit from a member of the house of Bedford, Henry Robin Ian Russell, the Marquess of Tavistock, when making a short visit to Tavistock. Robin Russell was to succeed his father in 2002 and become the 14th Duke of Bedford, a title that was held only for one year terminating in his early death in 2003.

The Duke's Diary

Put Some sparkle into your Year, come and Join Us at **THE BEDFORD HOTEL**. We are catering for all tastes. So there's bound to be something for you and your family in our Calendar of Events.

February
VALENTINE'S DINNER DANCE
Saturday 13th February 1988.
OUR Romantic candlelit 4 course dinner £13.50 per person.
VALENTINE'S 4 COURSE SUNDAY LUNCHEON
14th February 1988
TREAT your other half and enjoy our special luncheon. £7.95 per person
Try our Tasty Pancakes on SHROVE TUESDAY.
Served all day 16th February 1988.
Friday 12th February — Sunday 24th March.
SPECIAL liqueurs and liqueur coffee promotion.

March
MOTHERING SUNDAY
Sunday 13th March
SPECIAL luncheon. Happy Les the Clown will make you laugh. £8.50 per person.
GREEK EVENING —
Saturday 26th March
£14.50 per person. inc Entertainment & VAT.

April
BEST OF BRITISH PROMOTION
8th April to 19th May.

EASTER BANK HOLIDAY LUNCHEON
£7.25 per person inc VAT,
HAPPY Les the Clown will entertain you!
Saturday 23rd April
ST GEORGE'S DAY BANQUET
MEDIEVAL £14.50 per person inc VAT.

May
BANK HOLIDAY LUNCHEON
Monday 2nd May 1988
£7.25 per person
HAPPY Les the Clown will entertain you!.
Children only £3.50
AROUND THE WORLD IN 4 COURSES
Saturday 21st May.
SPECIALITY Dinner £14.50 inc VAT. Something Different!
MAY BANK HOLIDAY LUNCHEON
Monday 30th May.
£7.25 per person. Happy Les The Clown will entertain you! Children only £3.50

June
MEDITERRANEAN PROMOTION
starts 10th June - 21st July.

MIDSUMMER NIGHT'S DREAM DINNER DANCE
Saturday 18th June
£14.50 per person
Sunday 19th June
it's FATHER'S DAY! Special Dad's Luncheon £7.75.
Children only £3.50
WIMBLEDON TEA PARTIES —
Monday 20th June to 3rd July.
We will serve!

July
ARMADA DINNER
Saturday 23rd July
To celebrate 400 years. Deluxe Menu £16.50 per person.

August
SPECIAL SUMMER LUNCHEON PLATTER
5th August to 29th September.
SEAFOOD GOURMET NIGHT
Saturday 27th August
£14.50 per person
AUGUST BANK HOLIDAY LUNCHEON
Make it a family treat! £7.25 per person.

September
60's NIGHT
Saturday 17th September —
COME and remember the old days!. £14.55 per person.

October
FRENCH PROMOTION
14th October to 24th November.
Halloween —
TRICK OR TREAT —
Monday 31st October.
Dinner Dance — well it's really a treat!

November
Saturday 5th GUY FAWKES NIGHT
Come to our BBQ and Banger evening!
£4.95 per person -children only £2.50.
BEAUJOLAIS NOUVEAU Arrive!
Thursday 17th November.
BEAUJOLAIS SPECIALITY DINNER
Saturday 19th November. £14.50 per person.

December
CHRISTMAS FAYRE MENU
Starts 5th December 1988.
Saturday 10th December —
Hotel Xmas Party Night.
Friday 16th December —
Hotel Xmas Party Night.
Saturday 17th December
Hotel Xmas Party Night.
Wednesday 21st December Hotel Xmas Party Night.
Saturday New Year Candlelit Dinner Dance £29.50 per person

Accommodation Special Rate, B & B £25 Double, £15 Single, subject to availability

If you would like further information about any of these events, please indicate those in which you are interested and return this card to the Bedford Hotel, Plymouth Road, Tavistock. Or call us on Tavistock (0822) 3221.

Trusthouse Forte Hotels

Book now to save disappointment.

Bedford Hotel diary of events for 1988

Advertisement for a lobster special 1988/9

Head Chef Willie Stephens with a rather disgruntled lobster – possibly suffering from jet-lag after his flight from New England but maybe knowing what's for lunch

Under manager James Lever the kitchen area underwent a £41000 refit c1987 and the speciality events continued and he managed to get wide publicity in the local press with frequent photographic opportunities for publicity. James was, however, another short stay manager, moving to pastures new within the THF Group in 1988

It was in James Lever's 'time' that the Bedford Hotel was again commissioned to provide a luncheon for the visit of Royalty, in this case the Prince Edward who came to Tavistock to open the new Meadowlands Pool on 23rd July 1988. Posh Nosh was again provided and chefs Chamings, Couch and Stephens had a second chance to get a chef's post at the Palace. Despite the excellence of the food no such opportunities were forthcoming.

John Barker became the next man in charge; he was to stay for some 8 years. In John's 'reign' an important historical event was to be part celebrated in the hotel in 1994 when officers of the 29th US Infantry Division returned to Tavistock to rekindle the friendship and admiration which had grown between locals and the American forces stationed in Tavistock prior to D-Day in 1944 when the Division embarked for Omaha Beach. The celebrations were sealed with the presentation of the Colours of the Division being presented to Tavistock, and these currently hang in the Town Hall, a proud reminder of Tavistock's importance in World War 2 and the close affinity of the town with the 29th Division.

In 1992 the local Borough Council voiced a scheme to incorporate the vicarage garden and the Bedford Hotel car park into an enlarged borough car parking facility. However, there was a

John Barker and staff displaying the flag of the White Hart Hotels Group,
formed as part of THF group in 1995

rethink on behalf of the Borough Council Planning Department and a statement appeared in the local press concerning the proposal upon the discovery by the Planning Department that this was an ancient site and should, perhaps, be treated with respect. Scheme dropped.

By 1986 the Bedford Hotel had become part of the Forte Heritage Group but further major business restructuring within the THF group of companies meant the Bedford Hotel becoming part of the White Hart Hotels, a subsidiary of THF, in August 1995. It is not clear what benefit, if any, came to the Bedford Hotel in Tavistock as a result of this move, but they did get a shiny new flag.

At some time in the 1990s the decision was taken by the Forte Group to close the Bedford Bar and convert it into the Foulston Room This was considered to be an act of gross maladministration by a certain set of Tavistock folk who had used this venue for years as a quiet, comfortable and homely place for the middle classes to visit with their friends and enjoy the ambience of the place. So furious were these Bedford 'groupies' that a poem was written to voice their disgust.

<u>"On the passing of the Bedford Bar</u>

Tinto, Williams, Perry, Gozzard,
Nowhere now for them to drink
No more heard the cry for Plymouth
Gin and Lots of Ice, with Pink.
Will the ghost of the Commander
Haunt the function room they build?
Will the shade of Philip Perry
Weep at all the trade they've killed?
Beer gives way to instant coffee
Held in cups with fingers crooked;
Ladies' luncheons, slimmers' dinners,
Frozen fish cakes badly cooked.
Whiting in a van from Walsall;
Bread baked several weeks before;
Portions which are fixed and tiny,
No one ever asks for more.
Soon they'll have a robot barmaid;
Soon you'll have to pay to pee.
Soon the guests will do the dusting,
Soon the staff will cease to be.
Meanwhile, up in Mayfair gloating
As he counts his grisly loot;
Rocco gives his loyal barmaids
Notice that they've got the boot.

Sadly it's the same old story
Some grow fat on others' toil
Come the revolution Rocco

Should be fried in boiling oil.
This would be a fitting finish
For a chap we locals think
B------d up, all things considered
Quite a decent place to drink."

Williams was Major Williams, referred to as 'the Commander' and Philip Perry was part of the very well known Perry family of Tavistock and who was also a lifelong thespian making regular appearances with the Tavonians.

One cannot but feel that, although the frustration at the loss of a favourite drinking hole was deeply felt, Forte Group were certainly not all bad. The Group had shown a level of staff involvement and training which many companies of today should envy. As CEO of the Forte Group Rocco Forte's personal involvement in the presentation of achievement awards to trainee chefs and the like, is an open demonstration of the top man's belief that staff do matter, a management skill and commitment seen less and less today.

In its latter days the Bedford Bar was the responsibility of Sally Dodd and Lisa Hair, trainee managers at the time, but changes to the hotel's ownership and management were nigh.

The internal restructuring of the Forte Group in 1995 may have been a planned move by Forte as the forerunner of a 'sell-off' of hotels within the group but such is difficult to say due to the hostile takeover of Forte by Granada in January 1996. In May 1996 the Bedford Hotel was sold to Regal Hotels, part of the Corus Group, as part of a £121.7m move when Regal purchased 65 Forte Hotels from the old Forte White Hart Group: this made Regal one of the leading hotel groups in the UK owning some 117 hotels in the UK. The Regal statement read

> "As a collection of individual hotels, Regal encourages its properties to operate independently, working with the local community and offering the guests a friendly and personal service while the group offers sales, marketing and operational support, and invests in ongoing maintenance and redecoration."

Unfortunately such fine statements of intent sometimes fail to be delivered and over the next three years the Bedford Hotel went into a steady decline both in its restaurant and in its upkeep of the premises. Possibly the hotel suffered from being branded within a corporate whole such as Corus where there was a central menu bank and the purchase of local produce was not permitted – the latter certainly being against the historic trend for the Bedford which very much encompassed local supplies of both produce and labour; such practices of Regal also hardly demonstrated the claimed independence and working with the local community. Perhaps, too, some of the decisions made by the first manager for Regal, Susan Cadogan-Smith, were not in the interests of a local hotel such as the Bedford and during her tenure many organisations and individuals, including many of the staff members, ceased to be satisfied with the services offered. Following Mrs Cadogan-Smith's move some 18 months after the Regal takeover, there followed a period under the temporary management of Sally Dodd leading to the arrival, as permanent manager, of Mervyn White, in July 1998. Here was a man with the customer at heart, who, despite protestations from the Amalgamated Union of Geese, offered multi-forms of goose on Goose Fair Day; goose dinners in the bar or 'posh' goose sandwiches, rolls and curries etc; something which had been lacking at recent Goose Fair days in the town. Despite what was, perhaps, a valiant personal effort of the new manager, Tavistock was in serious danger of losing its prestigious historic hotel through apparent lack of tender loving care and support of the parent company.

There was, however, one small but notable exception to the disappointing days of Regal and that was the insistence of the CEO of Regal, Nicholas Crawley, that the magnificent oil painting in the hotel foyer be professionally restored and today this magnificent artwork proudly welcomes guests and visitors to the hotel. Good news, however, is often accompanied by bad; the bad news being that all the other antique works of art in the hotel were removed from the hotel, never to be seen again.

Notwithstanding art lovers, and despite amalgamations and buy-outs involving Regal and the Corus Group, the downhill slope could not be continued and in June 1999 Regal Hotels announced that the Bedford Hotel, as part of a group of some 34 hotels within Corus, was being disposed of because this internally owned group of hotels 'did not fit in with the Corus project'. The Corus Group was looking to concentrate on corporate business and was disposing of those smaller hotels that focussed on the leisure business. At the time of the announcement the Bedford Hotel was said to employ 28 staff and had 30 bedrooms.

The announcement by Regal offered an opportunity for the Bedford to regain some of its long held dignity and pride. New blood, new ideas, new money and new enthusiasms were needed and the twenty-first century was to see this hotel return to private ownership from the hands of big business that had seemingly failed to keep up the standards and success enjoyed for some 130 years from 1822 to 1955. Enter Mr Philip Davies.

Advertisement 1

Morning Coffee
Bar Snacks
Business Lunches
Sunday Lunches
Afternoon Teas
Private Parties

... or just dining out!

The

Bedford Hotel

Tavistock

Looks forward to welcoming you

Select the menu to suit your taste and pocket

For example:
*Avocado filled with cream Stilton
moistened with a raspberry coulis (£2.95)
Beef Stroganoff with a
timbale of wild rice (£5.95)
Fruits of the Forest shortcake with
Sauce Anglais (£2.95)*

For bookings please telephone 01822- 613221

REGAL

A Collection of Individual Hotels

Advertisement 2

Friends and relations visiting for their summer holidays ? We can help!

The

Bedford Hotel

Tavistock

is offering a special

Bed and Breakfast

rate of

£28.50 per person per night

during July and August 1998

and

on presentation of this leaflet

10 % off dinner

for two people staying at *The Bedford*
during July and August 1998

For bookings please telephone 01822- 613221
quoting VF BED

Subject to availability; Limited number of rooms available

REGAL

A Collection of Individual Hotels

The Regal Hotels' advertisments 1998

The Twenty First Century – A New Dawn for The Bedford Hotel

Mr Philip Davies had long envied THF and Regal Hotels in their ownership of this great hotel and on 22 September 1999 he bought the property and the business. The sequence of events leading to this new venture for Mr Davies was along similar lines to the gentleman who purchased the shaver company because he liked the product. After 130 years in the ownership of the Bedford family followed by some 40 years in the hands of the big hotel companies this hotel was to return to private ownership – what an opportunity.

Philip Davies was born, of Welsh parents, in Newark, Nottinghamshire, in the autumn of 1945. From the account above the majority of entrepreneurs who took on the lease of the Bedford Hotel as it stands today had 'beer in the blood', many coming from long established lines of families involved in the drink trade. Philip Davies is not in this mould. He is teetotal and, if anything, he has 'printer's ink in the blood' having been obsessed with all things printing since the age of 10, helped along by the fact that his father was involved in the printing trade with the *Surrey Mirror*. It was when working with the *Woking News and Mail* that Philip met his wife-to-be, Lesley, in 1963. Subsequently, from 1974 to 1979, Philip was in charge of Guardian Special Reports and over the years became a newspaper and magazine publisher in his own right eventually owning some 19 titles, covering the Isle of Wight to Carlisle. Many of these titles he eventually sold and began a 'second career' in hotel management although, today, he still owns, among others, the *Woking News and Mail* which was purchased from Guardian Newspapers in 2011.

Philip Davies's first hotels were one in Dunoon and one in Torquay, bought as a pair from the Cooperative Society, and neither of which he owns today. In 1982 Lesley and Philip moved from their home in Farnham, Surrey, to Chagford and a passionate affair with Dartmoor and surrounds rapidly grew and the hunt for a new hotel was on. The first Devon acquisition was the Two Bridges Hotel on Dartmoor, purchased in 1990, followed by the Bedford Hotel in Tavistock in 1999. When asked why he bought these two establishments he smiles when calmly revealing he bought the Two Bridges initially because he liked the picture of the hotel shown in an Estate Agent's window in Carmarthen. With regards to the Bedford the response was simple "I love Tavistock and adore the Bedford – they are two outstanding gems set in a crown of genuine beauty".

The Bedford's new owner has stood in three General elections and 'come second each time'. Now such could drive a man to drink but Philip did the next best thing – he became co-founder of the Dartmoor Brewery, Princetown, and now makes barrels full of beer but stoically resists the temptation. With excellent beers such as Dartmoor's Jail Ale and Legend freely on tap it is likely that the resistance to partake would be beyond the call of most.

Now that the Davies family were the owners there were the promises to 'restore it to its former glory', to refurbish and make it attractive and to give 'the town what they want'. They announced 'immediate plans' which included installation of a grand piano, cobbling the car park and installing a fountain at the back of the hotel – the piano is in place, the beautiful stone fountain, although purchased, requires shrinking in order for it to fit in where it was intended to go and is currently 'on holiday' away from the hotel site in the Davies's very large back garden. Cobbling of the car park will possibly be a sequel to the work undertaken on the new Gallery 26 Restaurant although, perhaps, 'elf 'n' safety' may intervene regarding the cobbling.

Mr Davies also announced "I'm giving family ownership and all that entails …" and, in line with an apparent Bedford Hotel tradition,

> " … a policy of buying everything locally – local foods, local suppliers. We aim to offer comfort, informality and friendliness."

Mr Davies obviously meant business. Within eight months of purchase the Bedford Hotel had been redecorated and the restaurant had been awarded AA Two Red Rosettes. However, life was not all a breeze and hotel spokeswoman, Jane Waters, in May 2000 claimed that the hotel was "desperately trying to recruit staff – we're so busy. But we are having difficulties finding the right people".

Apart from the appearance of the Mad March Hare the public face of the hotel remains remarkably unchanged after 190 years when viewed from the north-east and after some 100 years when viewed from the north-west.

The Mad March Hare atop the old billiard room 2010

The Bedford Hotel from the NE, 9 November 2009

From the opening of the Davies's hotel the senior management structure was Philip Davies, Managing Director, Michael Healing, Operations Director and Peter Cliff as Finance Director with John Whittle as the general manager. Today the hotel has Simon Rowe, as general manager and a total permanent staff of 35. Michael Healing, the Operations Director, retired in 2012.

The Bedford Hotel from the NW, 9 November 2009

It was Michael Healing who had the pleasure and frustrations of the development of the new function room, Gallery 26, a wonderful blend of medieval and modern architecture carried out with great sensitivity. This new room, which opened in 2010, was situated above the rear courtyard of the hotel. It was designed by Tavistock architect Stephen Whettem and involved extensive discussions with English Heritage and the Exeter Archaeology unit. During alterations for the new restaurant remains of medieval fabric were uncovered together with a portion of a surviving Wedgwood plate c1820 that was embedded in the C19 fabric of the walls at the rear of the hotel. Gallery 26 stands on stilts above the original yard of the 1725 Abbey House. Its construction involved demolition of a very ugly addition to the hotel (c1920s?) to the south of the reception desk and removal of a fire escape. The latter revealed a medieval window opening which now has pride of place alongside a C16 window opening, both part of the Abbey buildings, with C20 windows above cleverly decorated with 'stained glass'. And why Gallery 26? Philip Davies's birthday falls on the 26th day of the month – that's why.

Courtyard walls showing medieval arched openings and an open C19 window – 1m scale

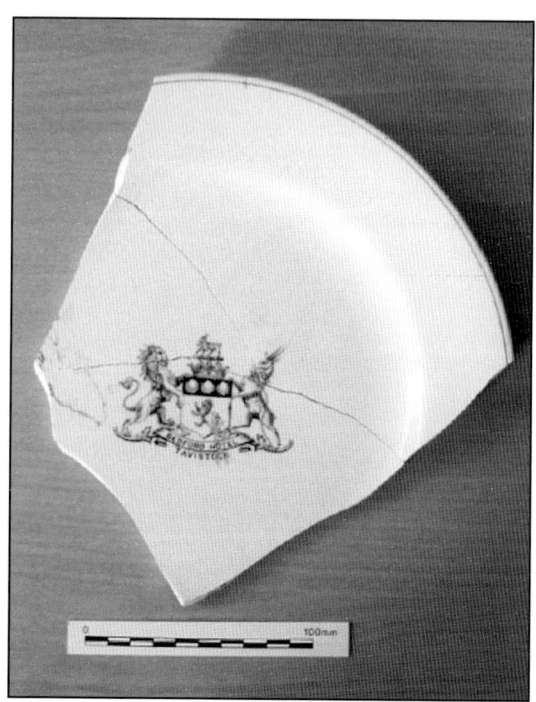

Wedgwood plate c1820 showing the arms of the Duke

Slate cladding (at fire escape platform) covering medieval window now incorporated into Gallery 26 – 2007

The old Smoking Room (later the Office) and fire escape in inner yard both removed to make way for Gallery 26 – 2007

South end of Gallery 26 at the west end showing surviving wall fabric of the Abbot's Lodging of Tavistock Abbey with a medieval window bottom, right, a C16 window bottom left and five upper windows of later date

Since 2000 the hotel has also benefited from the provision of modern, stylish toilet facilities, provision of private dining and conference facilities in the Portrait Room (formerly the Bedford Bar area) and the refurbishing of laundry storage and a small bedroom opposite reception to

Gallery 26 looking to east end with view over the Abbey Chapel

Relaxing with The Daily Telegraph, 2009 – oh, the bliss of an inn

provide the Tavistock Room which is used for conferences and silver service dining. In addition a bit of humour and colour has been added in the placement of stained glass door headings on the ground floor announcing Gallery 26, the Tavistock Room, the Devil's Kitchen etc.

The hotel provides the ambience and comfort of a good inn with fine kitchen backed up by menus for all tastes and good beer and wine – heaven is not far away. Conferences, auctions, private

Lunch is nearly served, 2009

parties, charity events and special evenings of music and romance are the norm. It is very hard in a history of this kind to resist pictorially representing the offerings of a fine inn and in showing the updated main facilities – so we will not so resist.

A busy kitchen, 2009

Charity Fashion Show in 2009 in Gallery 26

*The Russell Room in 2012. This was originally the reception area for the 1830s ballroom
which was accessed via two doorways either side of the fireplace on the left. The wall to the right was
added at a later date to provide a corridor to what is now the Portrait Room.*

The Reception Desk in 2012

The bar in 2012

The Portrait Room looking west in 2012

The main dining rooms in 2012 and showing the original 1725 ceiling plasterwork

The Bedford hotel has moved with the times, albeit oft time slowly, so it may well be asked "what is the next project?" Beginning in the summer of 2012 it is planned to install easy access to the hotel for all via the car park. As well as new stairs and lift access to the buildings the car park area will be visually enhanced by the removal of the rear fire escape and opening up of the area immediately under the ballroom to 'show off' the fine ancient granite columns which formed part of the access way to the 1830's ballroom.

In March 2012 the hotel employs some 35 direct staff (a mix of full time and part time), most of whom, including Philip Davies, were very shy about having their photographs taken. However, no hotel functions well without excellent staff and how often is the opportunity taken in the documented history of our English inns to record not only the names but also the likeness of all those who make such a complicated business work so well.

Today Tavistock can, as always, be proud of its number one hostelry. Let us raise our glasses to the Bedford Hotel and to the next 300 years.

The senior team at the Bedford Hotel, June 2012.
L to R – Simon Rowe, manager; Sarah Howard, hotel ambassador; Philip Davies, owner

The Bedford Hotel Staff, March 2012

Standing L to R – Jessica Hillier (waitress), Maria Tratten (bar supervisor), Lyne Evans (chef), Alice Evans (chambermaid), Clive Sloley (maintenance), Dylan Malford (food and beverage manager), Ashley Spilee (kitchen porter), Jordan Swinney (waiter), Sarah Howard (hotel ambassador), Kirsty Falconer (restaurant supervisor), Samny Voisey (chef)

Seated L to R – Nicole Fabienne Murry (waitress), Matthew Carder (head chef), Jane Askew (sales and marketing manager), Emma McKinnon (sales and events coordinator), Simon Rowe (general manager), Robynne Honey (receptionist), David Gee (housekeeper), Nina Harding (chef)

Aerial view of the Bedford Hotel – winter 2011

The Bedford Tap, Tavistock

The presence of a Tap is noted as early as 1823 when Thomas Rowe, victualler, is given as running the "Hotel Tap". This was the Bedford Tap that was located under the main entrance to the hotel and was used by the coachmen, ostlers and servants ie the Public Bar as opposed to the Saloon or the Lounge. No further trace of Thomas Rowe has been found – that's what strong drink does.

Also no further trace of the Bedford Tap itself is found in contemporary directories and the decennial census returns have been found to be the prime source for the men and women of the Bedford Tap together with newspaper obituaries in the twentieth century. John and Mary Cole, both born c1815, ran the Tap from at least 1850 through to 1871. It is probable that John combined the Tap with his job as an ostler, ably assisted in the bar by Mary. Devon born of Jacobstow John and Mary Cole lived out their days in Tavistock. By 1881 John was given as a retired publican aged 66 living at No 2 Abbey Mead in Tavistock with wife Mary. He died in Abbey Mead on the 25th of March 1886 and Mary died on 26th February four years later. They rest together in Plymouth Road Cemetery.

On John Cole's retirement the new Tap man was Tavistock born Simon Webber and his wife Elizabeth from Peter Tavy. Simon's earlier career had included that of a lead miner in Christow in 1861 and copper mine engine driver whilst living in Calstock in 1871. A change of career to Bedford Tap barman was in place by census 1881 and it is likely that Simon would have taken over in the 1870s when John Cole retired. Simon died of kidney problems and oedema in the Bedford Hotel Tap in November 1887, he was aged 59 and is buried in Peter Tavy churchyard. Elizabeth was to remarry in 1890 to a Samuel Radmore, a retired farmer. They lived at Kilworthy Hill in Tavistock and Elizabeth died in October 1903 at 2 Church View, Whitchurch, aged 76, and is also buried in Peter Tavy, with her first husband Simon.

A new entry as manager of the Tap is found in 1891 when Edith Burgoyne is given as 'tap manager' at the Bedford, where her husband John was 'head boots', Edith having taken over the Tap from the Webbers. Torquay born Edith was just 25 and her husband, from Crediton, was 29. By 1901 no trace of this pair has been found in England or Wales.

In 1891 Samuel Scown was a coachman living at 57 Bannawell Street with Tavistock born wife Sarah and three month old daughter Annie. Samuel was born in Lewannick in Cornwall. He married Sarah Ann Mills in E Stonehouse in the winter of 1890 and by 1901 census he was a yardman in the Bedford Hotel and his wife was manageress of the Bedford Tap – most probably a husband and wife team in the bar also. In the spring of 1904 William Northcott of the Union Inn, in King Street, died and Samuel Scown removed from the Bedford Hotel to take over the

Union until its rebuild in 1913/14, by which time, likely from 1912, he had taken on the Temperance Hotel in Pym Street which he was to run as Scown's South Western Private Hotel (now the Ordulph Arms). On the death of the new incumbent of the Union Hotel Samuel Scown took over the inn for a second time until October 1927, followed by refreshment rooms at 5 King Street (1930 to 1935). Samuel died in Tavistock aged 84 on 2 December 1947 having lived in Tavistock for some 60 years. It is said that Samuel's lifelong interest was hunting and for many years he was the Whip to Mr Spooner's Harriers and on occasion hunted the pack. He was also one of the oldest members of the Tavistock Conservative Club and a member of the Ancient Order of the Foresters and also the Royal and Ancient Order of the Buffaloes. Sarah had predeceased him at the age of 72 in March 1938 and they lie together, with Sarah's mother Mary Mills, in Plymouth Road Cemetery.

Whilst it is not suggested that Scown run a disorderly house enjoyment was the name of the game and occasionally the swift arm of the law caught up with those who had over-indulged. Whether it was a greater privilege to be caught "d and d" after drinking at the Bedford Tap, rather than the Crown or the Ordnance Arms etc, is possible but, in August 1893, one of Tavistock's more persistent, and possibly more colourful, drunks, Charles Craze, decided that the Bedford was the place to go. Craze, a 24 year-old mason by profession, objected to the interference of the local bobby, PC Cox, and assaulted the poor fellow. The Bench, who three months earlier had advised Craze to become a teetotaller, took a dim view of his antics and gave him three weeks with hard labour. The more usual price for such misdemeanour was five shillings and costs, which the more placid Benjamin Hole paid in February 1894 for being drunk and disorderly in the Bedford Tap.

The 1911 census return for the hotel indicates the likelihood of Frederick William Tucker and his wife Susan Agnes, being the staff for the Bedford Tap. Frederick was born in Stonehouse in Plymouth in 1867 the son of William Tucker a leather dresser and his wife Elizabeth (nee Heydon). After their marriage in 1865 the couple lived for a short time in Liskeard before returning to Plymouth by 1881. Frederick has a strange range of experience to become a barman. In his early twenties he was a cabinetmaker, moving on ten years later to become an agent for the Clothing Club and a Preacher for the Wesleyan Church (teetotallers all). By 1914 the Tuckers had moved on to be replaced by the long serving Slatters.

William Robert Slatter was born in Shipton-upon-Stour in Worcestershire in 1882, the eldest son and one of twelve children of Birmingham born George, a brewer working in the Tavistock brewery in 1901; the family was not in Tavistock in 1891. As a boy William had worked for his father when the latter took over the management of the old Tavistock Brewery in Brook Street. 1901 saw William working as a brewer's drayman in Tavistock and he married Marian Chave in St Eustachius Parish Church, Tavistock, in 1903. In 1914 William took over as mine host of the Bedford Tap where he remained until his retirement in 1947. In the First World War he served in the RASC in Greece and Salonika, during which time his wife managed the bar. William was a first class marksman and a member of Tavistock Miniature Rifle Club. He had shot for Devon and had won the Bell medal and numerous other prizes and was a member of Tavistock Conservative Club. He died at 6 Browne's Bungalows, Tavistock, on 5 May 1952 having lived in Tavistock for over 50 years and run the Bedford Tap for 33 of those years with his wife Marian, known as Mame, who was the daughter of James Chave of Bannawell Street, one of the finest cricketers that Tavistock has ever produced; her mother ran the Commercial Inn in Tavistock which was situated on the site of Drake Road, the inn being demolished at the end of the 19th century to make way for the new road to Tavistock North railway station. Mame died 7 January 1955 aged 73.

Harry Roberts was to take over the Tap in 1947 on the retirement of William Slatter. He was the youngest of six surviving children born to William Roberts and Mary Ann, nee Simmons, of Tavistock. In 1914, at the outbreak of the First World War, the four boys enlisted, the eldest, James, in the navy and the others in the 5th Battalion of the Devonshire Regiment. Harry, at the age of 15 enlisted as a drummer boy, having recently been an apprenticed plumber to Messrs Nicholson and Hill of Tavistock. With her husband having died in May 1914 and with four boys on active, front line service in different parts of the world, Mary Roberts must have lived an emotionally nail-biting existence in Tavistock with her two daughters. In the event three of the boys survived the war, Robert, being killed in action, age 23, in Marfaux in France. After the war Harry married local girl Emeline Maud Doidge, known as 'Jane', in Tavistock in 1926;

Harry Roberts (right) pictured with his brothers
Robert (centre) and Bert (left) c1917

Jane was the daughter of Charlie Doidge the long-serving Bedford Hotel gardener. Harry was keenly interested in athletics and was said to be the mainstay of Tavistock Football Club – 'his skill made him one of the best players for many years'. For some time Harry and Jane had lived in Crownhill in Plymouth and Harry worked for many years as a plumber in Devonport dockyard. Their house was bombed, a direct hit, and Harry and Jane and their daughter Glenda survived care of an underground Anderson shelter erected in their garden by Harry. On being 'bombed-out' Harry and Jane returned to Tavistock where Harry worked for the plumbing firm of Cyril Holwill whose business was under the railway viaduct in Taylor Square. After living temporarily with his brother and family in Brook Street Harry took over the Tap.

According to their nephew Trevor James, Harry and Jane got to know almost every customer of the Tap by the boots or shoes they wore. The customers would enter the bar via the flight of stone steps alongside the entrance to the Bedford Hotel and as they entered for a beer or three Jane would observe the entry thus "Here's Bert" (or Henry or Bill as the case might be) she would say adding "he'll be wanting his pint of brown ale" (or whatever was his favourite tipple) and so it always happened that the man in question would be greeted by name with his drink waiting for him on the counter", reflecting the true duty of 'mine host'. Harry and Jane also ran a darts team, as most pubs did at that time. There was accommodation included for them on the premises and there Harry and Jane remained for many happy years.

Harry who was an acknowledged popular figure in Tavistock died at the early age of 53 on 13 November 1952 leaving the running of the bar to Jane, his widow. Jane remarried an Edward Francis Burley in St Eustachius's Church in 1962 and died on 9 August 1980 aged 80. She lies with her first husband Harry in Plymouth Road Cemetery and their infant daughter Brenda who died in 1931.

By 1976 the Bedford Tap had ceased to be run as a commercial 'Public Bar'. Meantime, in 1969 renewed attempts had been made to revive Tavistock Rugby Club. After a number of faltering starts the newly formed club, as well as playing on different, unsatisfactory, pitches, also lacked an HQ and, much more importantly, a bar that they could call their own. At the beginning of the 1976 season the Bedford Hotel agreed to the use of the ex Bedford Tap to be used as HQ and 'reviver premises' where battered, bruised and thirsty heroes could forgive the opposition all their misdemeanours, boast about their own prowess, slag off the referee, talk of love and sex, sing bawdy songs and generally enjoy themselves. The facility was staffed by Rugby Club officers and stocked through the auspices of the Bedford Hotel.

Despite the occasional problems between an organisation comprising very thirsty, very boisterous, very young, and often very thoughtless, rugby players, and, perhaps, occasionally their guests, the bar served as social HQ for the Rugby Club. To put the problems into context it does need to be remembered that after playing eighty minutes of rugby, showering and travelling back to the HQ, and bar, and then having to wait an hour for the bar to open under the then current licensing restrictions, such young men did tend to get rather eager for a pint or three with the opposition in order to forgive them of their sins. Problems between the licence holders, the Bedford Hotel, and the eager users of the ex Tap could not have been so bad as the arrangement lasted until the move of the Rugby Club to use the Cottage Inn in the mid-1980s and finally, on to Sandy Park after the formal opening of the new ground and HQ in 1991.

Since the move of the Rugby Club from the Tap the ex-bar was used for some ten years, from the mid-1980s to the mid 1990s, as a meeting room for the Tavistock Lions' Club following which it was in use as 'the new staff room' for the Hotel. Today, after standing forlorn – but still reflecting on its past glory days as Tavistock's number one public bar – this area is a flat housing staff of the hotel.

Regrettably, none of the Bedford Tap clientele appear to have stopped drinking for long enough to make a photographic record of this now long lost drinkers' paradise.

The Managers of the Bedford Hotel post – 1995

Ever since the take-over by the Trust Houses company in 1955 the hotel licence has been held by a nominated representative of the owning company and the hotel run by appointed managers from within the owning group.

At the re-opening of the Trust House hotel on 1 November 1955 the first managers were Mr and Mrs B J Dodridge, natives of Plymouth, who had previous assistant managerial experience at the Dartmoor Inn at Merrivale, followed by full managership of the Lansdowne Arms at Calne in Wiltshire. The Dodridges had a habit of 'always being down in the bar' and it would appear that, despite Mrs Dodridge's skill as a flower arranger, other skills were lacking. Her attempt to get the chef of the day sacked rebounded slightly and out went the Dodridges with 'one minute's notice' in April 1957; the chef just carried on cooking.

By the 15th of May 1957 Mr and Mrs Flanagan, previously from the Old Cock Inn, Harpenden, Hertfordshire, had taken over from the ejected Dodridges, The Flanagans were to stay for 4 years before taking a step up in the THF world and moving to the larger Imperial Hotel in Barnstaple in May 1961.

On 24 May 1961 a young married couple by the name of Roome were next in line as managers, coming to Tavistock from the Francis Hotel in Bath. They were said to be very hard workers and eventually moved to Buckfastleigh to run a restaurant. Their successor was an ex-army man and ex POW in Japanese hands. He in his turn was a very severe man with his staff and there were, apparently, few tears when he moved on to another THF establishment in Barnstaple; perhaps that is why none of the staff still around can remember his name; he was likely Michael Dolamore who moved from Hereford and took 'the seat' in October 1965.

By 1966 Geoffrey Stockman was in house and remained at the Bedford for some eight years. In 1971 he was responsible for overseeing the £45000 hotel facelift of that

Geoffrey Stockman

153

Eddie Loendawhl

John and Elizabeth Barker

year. Sheila Stoneman described Geoffrey Stockman as a very nice man whose life was, apparently, bedevilled by his own problems.

Geoffrey was followed by two short term incumbents over the period 1977 to 1979. Firstly, by Eddie Loendawhl and in October 1978 by husband and wife team John and Elizabeth Barker; who were to stay for less than a year.

John and Diana Strickland, another husband and wife team took over in July 1979 having

moved from a Trust House Hotel in Camberley in Surrey. John appeared to believe his strength was in the restaurant side of the business when he stated a desire to 'improve the standards' – well he had to say something.

In 1983 Graham and Sue Hutchinson were in charge for a few months only to be quickly followed by Rob Sullivan.

Rob Sullivan, 29, moved in in December 1983 previously having worked at the Castle Hotel in Windsor for two years, where he met his future wife Lyndsey, and at the Trust Houses Gloucester Hotel in London. At the Castle Hotel Mr Sullivan was food and catering manager and had experience of catering for royalty but likely not first hand fire fighting experience; within weeks of taking over Mr Sullivan had had to contend with a fire in the

John and Diana Strickland

154

hotel which damaged twelve rooms and a function room. However, Rob also had the pleasure of seeing receptionist Mandy Tugwell winning the Trust House Hotel Receptionist of the Year for 1983.

During his tenure Rob Sullivan urged the local Chamber of Commerce to 'adopt a positive attitude towards the future of the town and he himself instigated many new ideas into the Bedford including different one evening menus for the restaurant to include such variation as Mexican, Spanish, Greek, Caribbean etc as well as the locally sourced and named dishes. Add on also other zany ideas such as a Hippopotamus barbecue in the hotel garden in aid of NSPCC and a two-day package deal celebrating Christmas in the Summer. There is no doubt that this was a very popular manager and the staff commissioned an oil painting of the hotel, by local artist Arthur Reed, when Rob Sullivan moved on. He and his wife Lyndsey moved within the THF group in August 1986 to manage the 80 bedroomed, four star, Dudley Hotel in Hove.

James Lever took on the responsibility of the hotel in August 1986, moving in from the Mayflower Hotel in Plymouth his residency at the Bedford being a short two years only. However, James carried on themed evenings in the restaurant such as "Round the World: Four Courses" on 16 May 1987, all for £12-50.

Rob Sullivan

James Lever

The challenge of managing Tavistock's premier hotel was next taken up by the man from Sale. John Barker, aged 30, moved to Tavistock from his previous post as deputy manager at the Queen's Hotel, Chester, in John's own county of Cheshire, where his wife, Bryony, was banqueting assistant. John took over in November 1988 and his previous experience had been with THF in

John Barker   *Susan Cadogan-Smith*

Teesside, Dereham, and Oxford; he had also had experience working at the prestigious Palace Hotel in Paignton. Here, indeed, was a man of great wisdom and intellect professing his interests, apart from hotel management, to be local history, stamp collecting, chess and one foible, backgammon.

The first manager under Regal Hotels was Mrs Susan Cadogan-Smith a 40 year old lady who had previous experience as a trainee manager with THF, followed by public house management with Whitbread and then, some years later, running a filling station (petrol rather than beer) on the Isle of Wight followed by two years as deputy manager at a hotel in Tewkesbury. Mrs Cadogan-Smith had very forthright views about Regal having "an enlightened attitude to putting women in top posts" and that "ill-informed chauvinistic prejudice can still cross swords with enlightenment". She seemed strongly of the view that "men get intimidated by lady bosses – the older men especially ..." and that, as far as her own judgemental capacity was concerned, "... when you walk through the door you get the feel for a place. You know if you are going to like it or not. There is an ambiance that hits you in the face". When Susan gave these views to the local press in Tavistock she claimed to have enjoyed her first month at the Bedford and one presumes the 'ambiance' etc was right. Within six months she claimed she had been 'terrified' by ghostly presences in the hotel – likely members of that group of grumpy, bossy, sexist, unenlightened old men. Oh, and the ghostly apparition was a Cavalier, not a common or garden fellow, and the newspaper reports had no mention of whether Susan had been to a party the evening before the apparition appeared.

The early months with Regal were not to turn out to be the best period in the Bedford Hotel's history. Within a few months Mrs Cadogan-Smith moved on to elsewhere in the group and a temporary period of management was put in place under Sally Dodd who ran the hotel with the active help from others within Regal.

The temporary management arrangement under Sally Dodd gave way to Mervyn White who joined the Bedford as General Manager on 21 July 1998. He was to be the last manager of the Bedford Hotel under the ownership of the Regal Hotels and Corus Group. Mervyn had started in catering at the age of 14 scrubbing potatoes in the sergeants' mess at RAF Rissington. Leaving school he got his first proper job with Taylorplan Commercial Catering in the Shetland Isles, a post that lasted two years. In 1983 he joined Trust House Forte in the Posthouse brand as Head Waiter leaving three years later as Restaurant Manager. In 1988, after various other hotel posts Mervyn rejoined the Forte Group in the Forte Heritage arm as catering manager in the prestigious Plough and Harrow Hotel in Edgbaston later becoming Operations Manager within Regal Hotels and taking his first General Manager's position at the Bedford, a post he held until the Bedford changed hands in 1999. After the Bedford he remained with the Corus Group until 2002 when he started White Knights Ltd offering interim management service skills for many hotel groups. Mervyn's short term 'permanent stay' in the Bedford Hoptel awakened within him a love for Tavistock and his change of direction into self-employed consultancy enabled him to establish a real permanent home for himself and his family. At the time of writing Mervyn still lives in the town.

Mervyn White   *John Whittle*

In September 1999 Philip Davies and his wife procured the Bedford Hotel from Regal Hotels and the new general manager was Mr John Whittle. After a very short tenure John was followed into the chair by Simon Rowe.

Now the 'local hotel' was coming into being with a manager who was born in Tavistock and schooled in Callington. Somehow Simon was destined for the hotel trade. From the age of 15 he spent his time obtaining work experience in the once lovely Webb's Hotel in Liskeard. Formal training followed and included studying hotel and catering management in Camborne College. His initiation into the real world of catering was a two-year apprenticeship learning many disciplines of the trade in five different hotels including the Victoria in Sidmouth, the Chine in Boscombe and the Crown Hotel in Lyndhurst. The hard work really began from then on. Firstly, 10 years at that great Victorian hotel, the Duke of Cornwall in Plymouth, rising to senior assistant manager. A short term post at the Two Bridges Hotel on Dartmoor and a year at the Elford Lee in Plympton finally led to Simon becoming the manager of the Bedford Hotel in Tavistock in 2003 – welcome home Simon.

Simon Rowe

The Ghosts

Any self-respecting hotel of advanced years on an historic site, especially an Abbey site, has surely to have its ghost(s), or alleged ghost(s). The Bedford Hotel is no exception.

Jane Brown of Tavistock tells a most interesting tale about her parents who spent the second night of their honeymoon in the Bedford Hotel on the 4th of April 1952. Donald Milton, a solicitor, had married Barbara Rayner, a nurse, in Chelsea and the happy couple travelled by car to Tavistock and relaxed from the hustle and bustle of the day's events in the Bedford, a stop on their way to Fowey to complete their honeymoon. Whilst in bed the couple heard footsteps "walking purposefully down the corridor and stopping outside of the room." Donald 'leapt' out of bed and opened the door to find nobody there. However, there was nowhere else for a 'purposeful' being to go as the Miltons had a bedroom at the end of a corridor and there were no rooms opposite. The couple repeated their experiences to the staff next morning and were told that it was well known that a ghost frequented that corridor.

The very 'down to earth' and educated Miltons confessed all of their married lives to have been 'spooked' by this happening and often repeated the story without deviation of commentary to their friends, children and grandchildren even though Donald especially was a real sceptic for ghosts and the like.

Coincidentally, on the 28th of August 2011 Donald and Barbara Milton's granddaughter, Anna, spent a part of her honeymoon in the Bedford Hotel – but there are no reports of ghosts.

The *Tavistock Gazette* in May 1956 relates a story about the Ghost of Betsy Grimbal having been seen by former occupants of the Vicarage next door to the hotel. She is alleged to appear in the form of a grey or a black-robed lady, never as a white figure. (Betsy Grimbal, a lady allegedly murdered by a soldier in the ancient building between the hotel and the vicarage, is part of Tavistock folklore).

In May 1997 the then manager, Susan Cadogan-Smith, called in the services of a medium as described in the local paper, the *Tavistock Gazette.*

> "A medium has been called in to try to pacify an unhappy and restless ghost of a Cavalier which has been haunting the Bedford Hotel in Tavistock.
>
> Unexplained happenings including lights being turned on and off and furniture being moved during the night have upset and frightened the staff.

General manager Susan Cadogan-Smith said: The hotel has always had ghosts – Betsy Grimbal, a young girl who was murdered by a monk, haunts the reception area but she has never worried us. But since I moved here six months ago many more things have occurred and over Easter I had a frightening experience as I worked in my office during the early hours of the morning. I saw shadows pass my door and suddenly felt terrified – the air felt heavy and I couldn't move. I have never been so frightened in my life.

International medium Ann Cairns from Calstock met the Cavalier who haunts the top floor during a visit to the hotel last month and returned this week to soothe the soldier. 'This ghost was causing Susan a lot of problems' Ann Cairns said. 'He was not unhappy with the changes she has made to the hotel but I sorted him out. He was not harmful and I made him a little happier and I think he will go away now. I feel he lost his children here and he was entombed after a member of his family informed on him.

There are lots of presences in the hotel. A Victorian lady with a large bunch of keys showed herself to me but she was a very happy woman.'

Room seven has also caused the staff to feel a little uneasy. Susan Cadogan-Smith explained ' ... I was there one night and had a terrible nightmare ... Ann Cairns went into the room and got out her pendulum. The pendulum started spinning and then she described my nightmare although I had told only one other person about it.

Guests have seen the Cavalier walking along the corridor in his white nightshirt and I had to tell them there were no other people staying in the hotel that night. There have been so many unexplained happenings recently that I will be happy if Ann can stop the Cavalier wandering about."

One is very tempted politely to suggest to Mrs Cadogan-Smith that perhaps she should take a little more water with it and, of course, her superiors would hardly fail to notice from the press report that she worked until the 'early hours of the morning'. As a consequence of Mrs Cadogan-Smith's sterling work on improving the hotel, the company could look forward to many future bookings from happy, satisfied Cavaliers. Perhaps one should also enquire as to how the unsuspecting observer knows that the 'thing' wandering about in a white night shirt was a Cavalier.

Bedroom manager David Gee has been at the Bedford for some 37 years. Whilst not having seen an apparition, he has, on a number of occasions, been somewhat perturbed by 'a cold presence'. When joining the hotel in 1974 the young 17 year-old David had been warned about the hotel ghosts.

Chambermaid Ruth Lavers had not previously been told of any ghosts being seen in the hotel but tells stories of her own experiences of a 'ball of light', of windows closing, of lights and televisions being switched on after staff have turned them off, of 'a cold presence' and of the fact that some rooms are more notorious than others for 'the presence'. Whilst Ruth has only been at the hotel since November 2008 she is adamant that she has seen a woman in Victorian-like dress, walking down the first floor corridor and a man dressed in a top hat and black hair down to his shoulders near room 37; this latter event immediately after keys in the door had mysteriously rattled with 'no-one there'.

In the 1990s Sally Dodd, now working on the local newspaper after her time working at the Bedford offers her knowledge of the ghosts and alleged ghosts as follows

> "There was supposedly a ghost of a child … This was from when there was a school on that site, and a plague came to Tavistock, the cries heard were supposed to be from suffering children. Many staff heard this as this was a sleepover room back in the old days. Also there is supposed to be a ghost of a housekeeper and a soldier in the room on the top floor … I believe the story is she killed him …"

Shirley Wallis, a friend of Sally Dodd and a medium of great repute, came to the hotel and went around to where staff and guests had supposedly seen and heard peculiar things and cleared the atmosphere.

In the early part of the 21st century a lady known to the then Operations Director, Michael Healing, was adamant that she was followed about by something 'a bit mysterious' – there is no knowing if she was disappointed if and when 'it' caught up with her.

Notwithstanding such seemingly outlandish suggestions the testimonials to unearthly presences still persist – whether those testifying had been previously alerted to ghostly events in the hotel before making their own observations is not known but the tales are interesting; make of these tales what you will but be frightened not as all the ghosts are now happy ghosts.

The Bedford Hotel and its surrounding buildings of recognised Architectural and Historical Importance

The present Bedford Hotel has a rich architectural and social history spanning nearly 200 years. As part of the ancient Tavistock Abbey site it is part of a Scheduled Ancient Monument and stands in one of the most attractive and enriched townscapes in Devon, and likely the UK, and the building itself is ennobled by the rich architecture of its immediate neighbours – everyone of its nearest neighbours is a Grade II, or above, listed building with the exception of a poor quality, insensitively designed public toilet block in Guildhall Square.

Since 1950 the Bedford Hotel itself has been classified as a Grade II Listed Building under the Town and Country Planning Act, thus confirming the historical and architectural importance of this building. Recent archaeological studies of the site and buildings were published by Blaylock in 1998 and 2001. Internally, the easily recognisable parts of Saunders's house of the early eighteenth century are in the dining room and the staircase adjacent

The 1950's listing for the hotel details the importance of the group value of the Bedford viz

> "The Bedford Hotel, the Vicarage, and Abbey Mead Nos 1 to 9, together with the buildings opposite (Nos 1 to 6 Bedford Place, Nos 10, 11 and 12 Abbey Mead and Abbey House, Russell Street), form the dignified layout, dating from the first half of the 19th century, at this end of Plymouth Road."

The latest official listing, in 1983, for the hotel reads

> "East end c1725, west end Mid C19 on the site of the monastic buildings south of the Cloisters of Tavistock Abbey. The east end was built as a dwelling house by Jacob Saunders. Two storeys and basement stone ashlar 5 bays. Exterior now has castellated parapets and mullioned and transomed windows converted from the c18 sashes circa 1820. The interior of this part retains an early C18 panelled dining hall and staircase. The west end was added by the Bedford Estate when the building was converted into a hotel in the middle of the C19. Three storeys stone ashlar in matching style with crenellated parapet and 6 bays and crenellated porch. Some slate hanging to the rear elevation."

What is clearly evident, from the works of Blaylock 1998 and 2001 and of Passmore 2010, is that the Hotel fabric incorporates surviving parts of stonework from Tavistock Abbey buildings. Also, whilst the datings within the listings for the hotel itself are not very accurate the listing firmly establishes the importance of the Bedford Hotel and its setting within Tavistock.

Standing in the porch entrance to the hotel and moving in a clockwise direction the following buildings are the hotel's next nearest neighbours – photographs are all taken on 9th November 2009 with the exception of the Bedford Dairy (Abbey Porch) which is now almost impossible to photograph from the front due to the recent building works for the new Gallery 26. However, the east façade of this building is clearly seen to the right of the Abbey Chapel below.

Betsy Grimbal's Tower was the western entrance to Tavistock Abbey precincts: mostly mid C15. Within the arch is a granite sarcophagus unearthed during the excavations for the Bedford Hotel; said to have contained the bones of Ordulf, founder of Tavistock Abbey. Listed Grade I: Scheduled Ancient Monument.

Betsy Grimbal's Tower

The Tavistock Vicarage, immediately west of the Bedford Hotel and Betsy Grimbal's Tower, Plymouth Road south side, was completed c1819 just previous to the remodelling of the Abbey House – listed Grade II.

Tavistock Vicarage

Numbers 2 to 12 Plymouth Road, north side, are very elegant Georgian properties, previously numbered as 1-6 at the time of the 1950 Listing. Number 2 was built pre 1831 but nos 4 to 12 were added in 1836. These buildings are said to be by Edward Blore (1786-1879), a renowned Georgian and Victorian architect who took over the building of Buckingham Palace when Nash was dismissed from that task. All buildings listed Grade II.

Nos 2 and 4 Plymouth Road

No 1 Church Lane is a small but distinguished Georgian house built in the neo-Grecian style said to be after the Plymouth architect John Foulston who was working for the Bedford Estate in Tavistock in the early C19. Circa 1825, listed Grade II.

No 1 Church Lane

The Abbey cloisters were on the south side of the Abbey Church, which was demolished over the period 1539 to 1700. The longer section of the L-shaped structure is the south wall of the Abbey Church and dates from. C13 – listed Grade I, Scheduled Ancient Monument.

The Abbey Cloisters

St Eustachius's is the parish church of Tavistock built on the proceeds of the cloth trade. Built in C14 and C15 and restored in 1844-1845 – listed Grade II.

Tavistock Parish Church of St Eustachius

The Town Hall was completed in 1863 and formally opened on the second of February 1864. It is built in the Gothic style to sit comfortably with the works of John Foulston in the neighbouring Guildhall Square – listed Grade II.

Tavistock Town Hall

The Weights and Measures Office was added to the western side of abbey gatehouse c1850. The original building was increased in size by approx 30% to the west between 1906 and 1922 – listed Grade II.

Former Weights and Measures Office

Court Gate is the ancient abbey gatehouse leading to the central Abbey Yard. This late C12 building has C15 additions and was restored by John Foulston in 1824 – listed Grade I; Scheduled Ancient Monument.

Court Gate with the former Weights and Measures Office on the left and the Subscription Library on the right

The Subscription Library and Librarian's cottage were both built in the late 1820s by John Foulston. Listed Grade II; these buildings, together with Court Gate, house the current Tavistock Museum.

Subscription Library and Librarian's Cottage with Police Station on the right

The Duke of Bedford statue is that of Francis, the seventh duke, and was erected by public subscription in 1864. It is made in bronze using copper from the nearby Devon Great Consols Mines, and is the work of Edward B Stephens. Listed Grade II.

Statue of the 7th Duke of Bedford

Police Station. Built in the 1820s in the Gothic style by John Foulston this is one of the earliest police stations in England. It incorporates an earlier C18 building known as Trowte's House and the group of buildings is listed Grade II*.

Tavistock Police Station and Trowte's house (on the right)

The War Memorial was erected by public subscription in 1921 and bears the names of 120 Tavistock men who gave their lives in WW1. In 1948 a scroll was unveiled recording the names of 39 men and one woman who gave their lives in WW2. Listed Grade II

Tavistock War Memorial

The Guildhall was opened in 1848 and is in the Perpendicular style. It was built by Theophilus Jones, architect and surveyor to the Duke of Bedford, on the site of former abbey buildings – listed in a group with adjoining buildings as Grade II*

Tavistock Guildhall

Abbey Bridge was built in 1763 for the new toll road joining the town centre to the Whitchurch Road. It was doubled in width in 1859/60 to accommodate increased traffic from the newly opened railway station. Listed Grade II.

Abbey Bridge

The West Devon Club was built as a private residence in the early half of C19 as part of the works in Guildhall Square. A Grade II listed building it is flanked on the south side by part of the Abbey wall.

The West Devon Club

The Post Office building was erected as a private residence in the early half of C19 as part of the works in Guildhall Square – listed Grade II.

Tavistock Post Office

The Abbey Chapel was part of the C15 early C16 Abbot's Hall and became a meeting place for dissenters in 1691. The arched doorway in the eastern elevation dates from 1845 – listed Grade II. **Porch to the Abbot's Hall** is a C15 or early C16 building which served for many years as the dairy to the Bedford Hotel – listed Grade I; Scheduled Ancient Monument.

Abbey Chapel and Porch (on the right)

The Bedford Chambers were built c1822 at the same time as the Abbey House was altered to serve as the Bedford Hotel. The Chambers served as the Duke of Bedford's Tavistock Estate Office until 1960 – listed Grade II.

Bedford Chambers

173

The Still Tower is a mediaeval building used by the abbey to distil herbs for medical purposes. The listed Grade II wall leading from the eastern elevation is part of the monastic wall. The Still Tower is listed Grade I; Scheduled Ancient Monument.

The Still Tower and Abbey walls

Appendix A

Tenure of the Owners, Tenants, Licence Holders and Managers of the Bedford Hotel – 1719 to 2009

Tenants of the Bedford Arms 1719 to 1821

John Smith	1719-1729
Thomas Babbidge	1741?-1745?
Mrs Hicks	1745-1747
William Skinner	1747-1757
David Depear	1757-1760
Richard Morris	1760-1768?
William Skinner	1768?-1775
George Cumberland Skinner	1775-1802
Ann Skinner	1802-1821

Tenants of the Bedford Hotel 1822 to 1955

John Truscott	1822-1834
John Taunton	1835-(1841)
Edmund Lakeman Elliott	(1843)-1849
William Rowe Northway	1849-1887
John Squire	1888-1904
Ellen Stanbury	1904-1910
William Isaac Lake	1910-1955

NB From 1926 until 1955 the Sansom Whites were managers of the Bedford Hotel for William Lake

Licence holders for Trust Houses and Trust House Forte Ltd

George F Dunn	1955-1962
John Marmaduke Ford	1962-1968
Gerald Glanfield Boyd	1968-1972
Jeremy D Logie	1972-1973
Gerald G Boyd	1973-1979
Michael D Finkleman	1979-1981

Owners of the freehold

The Duke's of Bedford	1719-1955
Trust House Forte	1955-1996

Regal Hotels   1996-1999
Warm Welcome Hotels   1999 ongoing

Managers for Trust Houses and Trust House Forte Ltd

Mr and Mrs B J Dodridge   1955-1957
Mr and Mrs E P Flanagan   1957-1961
Mr and Mrs Roome   1961-1965?
Mr and Mrs Michael Dolamore   1965
Geoffrey Stockman   1966? -1971?
Eddie Loendawhl   1977-1978
John and Elizabeth Barker   1978
John and Diana Strickland   1979-?
Graham and Sue Hutchison   1983
Rob Sullivan   1983-1986
James Lever   1986-1988
John Barker   1988-1996

Managers for Regal Hotels

Susan Cadogan-Smith   1996-1998
Sally Dodd   Jan 1998-July 1998
Mervyn White   July 1998-Sept 1999

Managers for Warm Welcome Hotels

John Whittle   Sept 1999-2003
Simon Rowe   2003-

Mine hosts of the Bedford Tap

John and Mary Cole   1851-1871+
Simon and Elizabeth Webber   <1881-1887
Edith and John Burgoyne   1887-1901?
Samuel and Sarah Scown   <1901?-1904
Frederick William Tucker   1911-1914
Wm and Marian Slatter   1914-1947
Harry and Emeline (Jane) Roberts   1947-1952
Emeline Maud Roberts (Jane)   1952-? (became Mrs Burley, and died 1962)
Tavistock Rugby Club HQ   1976 to mid-1980s
Tavistock Lions Club   mid-1980s to mid-1990s

NB Tenants for the missing dates have not been indentified.

Appendix B

Occupants of the Bedford Hotel on census nights of 1841 to 1911

Entries are as written and not corrected

FS – female servant   MS – male servant   Ind – Independent

1841

name	relation to head	marr status	sex	age	occupation	where born
Taunton John			m	46	innkeeper	not Devon
Taunton, Mary			f	43		not Devon
Taunton, Elizabeth			f	23		not Devon
Taunton, Grace			f	19		not Devon
Taunton, Juliana			f	17		Devon
Taunton, Josephine			f	16		Devon
Murch, Maria			f	25	FS	Devon
Davis, Elizabeth			f	12	FS	Scotland, Ireland or Foreign
Cann, James			m	30	ind	Devon
Snell, Thomas			m	35	ind	Devon
Cresswell, Edmund			m	28	ind	Scotland, Ireland or Foreign
Cockram, George			m	22	ind	Devon
Beazley, Hannaford			m	23	ind	Devon
Trigg, Robert			m	23	architect	Scotland, Ireland or Foreign
Lewin, William			m	20		Scotland, Ireland or Foreign
Wilkey, John			m	40	agent	Devon

1851

name	relation to head	marr status	sex	age	occupation	where born
Northway, William R	head	marr	m	42	innkeeper	DEV Tavistock
Northway, Sally	wife	marr	f	45		DEV Milton Abbott
Northway, Willam R	son	unm	m	7	scholar	DEV Tavistock
Goddard, Phillippa	serv	unm	f	20	house servant	DEV Beeralston
Lentern, Jane	serv	unm	f	28	house servant	DEV Bridestow

177

1851 (continued)

name	relation to head	marr status	sex	age	occupation	where born
North, Harriet	serv	unm	f	20	house servant	DEV Cullompton
Brewer, Mary A	niec	unm	f	16	dressmaker	DEV Holsworthy
Brewer, William N	neph	unm	m	13	scholar	DEV Holsworthy
Cook, Susanna	serv	wid	f	48	house servant	DEV Okehampton
Osborne, James	serv	unm	m	18	servant	DEV Drewsteignton
Knight, William	serv	unm	m	21	servant	DEV Tavistock
Down, Maria	serv	unm	f	25	house servant	DEV Bratton
Blake, George	visitor	unm	m	26	officer of Inland Revenue	SSX Chichester
Collins, Henry	visitor	unm	m	24	commercial traveller	Monmouth
Murchison, John H	visitor	unm	m	26	gentleman	Jamaica
Dean, Arthur	visitor	marr	m	44	civil engineer	Devonshire

In the Bedford Tap

name	relation to head	marr status	sex	age	occupation	where born
Cole, John	serv	marr	m	36	ostler	DEV Jacobstowe
Cole, Mary	wife	marr	f	36		DEV Jacobstowe

1861

name	relation to head	marr status	sex	age	occupation	where born
Northway, William R	head	marr	m	52	innkeeper	DEV Tavistock
Northway, Sally	wife	marr	f	55		DEV Milton Abbott
Northway, Mary R	dau	unm	f	24	assistant	DEV Tavistock
Northway, William R	son	unm	m	17	assistant	DEV Tavistock
Gillard, Mary	visitor	unm	f	45	lady	DEV Brixham
Hawkin, Richard	serv	unm	m	39	underboots	DEV Lydford
Knight, William	serv	unm	m	30	boots	DEV Tavistock
Symons, Charlotte	serv	unm	f	32	chambermaid	DEV Tavistock
Rowe, Louisa	serv	unm	f	25	waitress	CON St Blazey
Waterfield, Hannah	serv	unm	f	22	assistant	DEV Tavistock
Hard, Catherine	serv	wid	f	22	cook	DEV Lamerton

1861 (continued

name	relation to head	marr status	sex	age	occupation	where born
In the Bedford Tap						
Cole, John	head	marr	m	44	ostler	DEV Jacobstow
Cole, Mary	wife	marr	f	44		DEV Jacobstow
Dart, Susan	visitor	unm	f	42	dressmaker	DEV Jacobstow
Dinner, Flora A	scrv	unm	f	15	house servant	DEV Lamerton
1871						
Northway, William R	head	marr	m	62	hotel keeper	DEV Tavistock
Northway, Sally	wife	marr	f	65	hotel keeper's wife	DEV Milton Abbott
Northway, William R	son	unm	m	unm	land surveyor	DEV Tavistock
Slanderwick, Charles	visitor	marr	m	55	commercial traveller	DEV Tiverton
Beck, Henry	visitor	marr	m	52	commercial traveller	OXF Oxford
Wotton, Elizabeth G	serv	unm	f	36	general assistant	DEV Ermington
Venning, Ellen	serv	unm	f	21	servant kitchen maid	DEV Walfastisworthy
Lang, Elizabeth	serv	unm	f	27	servant cook	DEV Maristowe
Sussex, Mary J	serv	unm	f	20	servant chambermaid	CON Launceston
Simmons, Charlotte	serv	unm	f	40	servant chambermaid	DEV Tavistock
Rowe, Jane	serv	unm	f	19	servant waitress	DEV Tavistock
Cole, Sarah	serv	unm	f	20	servant waitress	DEV Tavistock
Percy, Simon L	serv	unm	m	16	underboots	DEV Inwardleigh
Knight, William	serv	unm	m	41	boots	DEV Tavistock
Nosworthy, Mary R	dau	wid	f	34	gentlewoman	DEV Tavistock
In the Bedford Tap						
Cole, John	head	marr	m	55	ostler	DEV Jacobstowe
Cole, Mary	wife	marr	f	55	ostler's wife	DEV Jacobstowe

1871 (continued)

name	relation to head	marr status	sex	age	occupation	where born
Dart, Susan	sis-in-law	unm	f	53	assistant	DEV Jacobstowe
Dart, Philip	lodger	marr	m	41	coach painter	DEV Jacobstowe

1881

name	relation to head	marr status	sex	age	occupation	where born
Northway, William R	head	widr	m	71	hotel keeper, farmer 100a empl 3 men	DEV Tavistock
Northway, William R	son	marr	m	37	hotel keeper	DEV Tavistock
Northway, Lucy J	son's wife	marr	f	25		DEV Christowe
Northway, William H J R	son's son	unm	m	1		DEV Tavistock
New, Mary A	asst	unm	f	50	barmaid	MID London
Snell, Jessie	serv	unm	f	27	under chambermaid	DEV Brentor
Sussex, Mary J	serv	unm	f	28	waitress	CON Launceston
Dawe, Thomas	serv	unm	m	25	underboots	DEV Milton Abbott
Webber, Simn	serv	marr	m	52	barman	DEV Tavistock
Webber, Elizabeth	serv	marr	f	52	barwoman	DEV Peter Tavy
Kenner, Mary R	serv	unm	f	22	kitchenmaid	DEV Beerferris
Lang, Emma	serv	unm	f	25	chambermaid	DEV Maristowe
Cole, Annie	serv	unm	f	21	nursemaid	DEV Marytavy
Bailey, Mary	serv	unm	f	18	waitress	DEV Tavistock
Knight, William	serv	unm	m	51	boots	DEV Tavistock

There is no separate entry for the Bedford Tap

1891

name	relation to head	marr status	sex	age	occupation	where born
Squire, John	head	marr	m	31	hotel proprietor and farmer	DEV Lamerton
Squire, Kate	wife	marr	f	32		LON Camden Town
Allman, John O	visitor	marr	m	45	commercial traveller	IRE Tralee
Kohler, Albert	visitor	unm	m	28	commercial traveller	WAR Birmingham
Wells, Frances M	serv	unm	f	28	assistant	YKS Seampston

1891 (continued)

name	relation to head	marr status	sex	age	occupation	where born
Peters, Mary E	serv	unm	f	41	cook domestic servant	DEV Devonport
Geak, Eliza	serv	marr	f	27	general servant	DEV Tavistock
Giles, Edith	serv	unm	f	22	kitchen maid domestic servant	DEV Tavistock
Allen, Ellen E	serv	unm	f	26	waitress domestic servant	CON St Austell
Mullen, Bessie	serv	unm	f	20	chambcrmaid domestic servant	DEV Tavistock
Burgoyne, Edith	serv	marr	f	26	Tap manager domestic servant	DEV Torquay
Burgoyne, John	serv	marr	m	29	head boots domestic servant	DEV Crediton
Bright, Richard	serv	unm	m	20	under boots domestic servant	DEV Stoke Gabriel
Collings, William R	serv	unm	m	17	billiard marker	DEV Torquay
Cawse, Robert	serv	unm	m	15	kitchen boy	DEV Wembury

There is no separate entry for the Bedford Tap

1901

name	relation to head	marr status	sex	age	occupation	where born
Squire, John	head	marr	m	47	hotel proprietor and farmer – employer	DEV Brentor
Squire, Kate	wife	marr	f	42		LON Camden Town
Mathews, Annie E	sister	marr	f	52	housekeeper (domestic)	DEV Brentor
Thomas, Alfred	visitor	widr	m	55	engineer (mining) – own account	GLS Gloucester
David, Henry	visitor	unm	m	56	commercial traveller – worker	KEN Greenwich
Tarbuck, Emily M	serv	unm	f	28	clerk hotel book keeper	STS Bloxwich
Jago, Bessie	serv	unm	f	27	general servant (domestic)	DEV Tavistock
Mullen, Mary A	serv	unm	f	26	general servant (domestic)	DEV Tavistock

1911

name	relation to head	marr status	sex	age	occupation	where born
Lake, William Isaac	head	marr	m	40	hotel proprietor	ESS Romford
Lake, Florence Mary	wife	marr	f	36		SRY Leatherhead
Lake, Doris Mary	dau	unm	f	12		DEV Plymouth

1911 (continued)

name	relation to head	marr status	sex	age	occupation	where born
Lake, Margaret Ellen	dau	unm	f	8		DEV Plymouth
Sawdy, Kathleen F F	visitor	unm	f	24	governess	DEV Devonport
Payne, Alice Elizth	serv	unm	f	36	housekeeper (hotel)	DOR N Chideock
Duffell, Amy	serv	unm	f	34	book keeper (hotel)	SRY Kingston
Tucker, Fredk William	serv	marr	m	44	barman (hotel)	DEV Stonehouse
Tucker, Susan Agnes	serv	marr	f	44	barmaid (hotel)	DEV Plymouth
Sinca?, Bessie	serv	unm	f	25	waitress (hotel)	CON Camborne
Whiteway, Bertha Ann	serv	unm	f	27	chambermaid (hotel)	DEV Plymouth
McCoy, Molly	serv	unm	f	20	pantrymaid (hotel)	IRL Co Mayo
Cowl, Arthur	serv	unm	m	19	billiard marker (hotel)	EGY Alexandria
Brooking, Herman May	serv	unm	m	18	underboots (hotel)	DEV Stokenham
Staddon, Isabella	serv	wid	f	50	cook (hotel)	LON Newington
Mooney, Lily Elizabeth	serv	unm	f	23	kitchenmaid (hotel)	LON Holloway
Gribbell, Ethel	serv	unm	f	22	chambermaid (hotel)	DEV Devonport
Gill, John Maunder W	boarder	unm	m	55	private means	AUS Moonbye
McLean, Joseph A	boarder	unm	m	63	ret wholesale draper	LAN Manchester
Price, Edith Blamira	boarder	wid	f	63		SCO Larges

Sources

The following is a summary of major documentary records consulted for this publication. Where a range of dates is given this does not indicate that each and item has been consulted within the range.

Internet and other unnamed sources have been used in many cases for inspiration and the revitalisation of a flagging brain and/or confirmation of some of the data. Such have not all been referenced below

<u>Tavistock Museum</u>

Anon; A Field Book to the Plan of Tavistock, 1751 to1752
Anon; Hurdwick Survey 1726

<u>Devon Record Office</u>

Anon; Register of Alehouse Licences; Q5 64/1 to 9, 1753 to 1784
Anon; Victuallers Recognisances,; QS65/7/1-7, 1822 to 1827
Anon; Quarter Sessions Records; 62/7/1-54, 1753 to 1822
Bedford Estate Deposit L1258, LP18, various bundles, 1757 to 1781
Bedford papers – Letters; W1258, 1746 to 1809
Bedford Papers – Rentals Books; T1258M, 1745 to 1840
Bedford papers; T1258M Devon; 67 (302) 1955
Parish Registers for Devon
Smith H; Tavistock Abbey Site Survey, 1726
Wynne J; A New Survey of the Borough of Tavistock, 1755

<u>Miscellaneous</u>

Anon; Prospectus for formation of United Plymouth Hotels Ltd, 1903 (West Devon Record Office)
Bedford Hotel Sale Catalogue; Humbert and Flint, London, 1955
Census returns for 1841 to 1911
Corderoy, Selby and Corderoy; Valuation for The United Plymouth Hotels Ltd, 1904
Last Will and Testament of Jacob Saunders 31 January 1738
Last Will and Testament of John Truscott proved 20 August 1834
Last Will and Testament of Thomas Edmund Elliott Administration dated 17 August 1850
Parish Registers; variously sourced and/or transcribed
Register of Licences for Tavistock Division; 1872 to 1880
Register of Licences for Tavistock Division; 1932 to 1981
Register Office for Births, Marriages and Deaths; 1837 to 2000
Stoneman S; private unpublished recollections of life in the Bedford Hotel, 1986

<u>Newspapers</u>

Exeter Flying Post, The 1775 to 1835
Plymouth, Devonport and Stonehouse Herald; 1848, 1849, 1850 and 1856

Tavistock Gazette; 1857 to 1974
Tavistock Times and *Tavistock Times Gazette* 1974 to 2009
Times, The 1823
Western Luminary, 1814
Western Daily Mercury 1869 to 1903

Published works

AA and RAC Members Handbooks; 1933 to 1976
Anon; Safety and Fire News, February 1984
Anon; The United Plymouth Hotels Valuation of 1904 (Plymouth Museum ref 2741/25)
Appleton, E; Transactions of the Devonshire Association for the Advancement of Science, Literature and Art; Part V, 122, Tavistock, August 1966.
Bedford John; A Silver Plated Spoon; Reprint Society, London, 1960
Blakiston, Georgiana; Woburn and the Russells; Constable, London, 1980
Blaylock S R; Tavistock Abbey, Devon; Assessment and Recording of the Standing Fabric; Exeter Archaeology, Rept 98.75, 1998
Blaylock S R; Tavistock Abbey, Devon; Further Recording of the Standing Fabric; Exeter Archaeology, Rept 01.82, 2001
Bray E A Mrs; Borders of the Tamar and the Tavy; Vol 1, 1879
Bray E A Mrs; Borders of the Tamar and the Tavy; Vol 3, 1879
Burritt E A; A Walk from London to Lands End and Back; 2nd Edition, London, 1868
Denham P V; The Duke of Bedford's Devon Estate 1820-1838; Rep Trans Dev Ass Advmt Sci, 110, 19, 1978
Evans R; Homescenes of Tavistock and its Vicinity; Greenfield, Tavistock, 1846
Finberg H P R; Tavistock Abbey; David and Charles, Newton Abbot, 1969
Freeman M and Wans J; Tavistock Abbey: Alternative interpretations; Rep Trans Dev Ass Advmt Sci, 128, 17, 1996
Giles B W; Tavistock's Methodist Chapels; Tavistock and District Local History Society, 2007
Gilpin W; Observations in the Western Parts of England; 1798 (republ by Richmond, 1973)
James, Trevor; Tavistock Memories; Amberley Publishing, 2010
John, Duke of Bedford; A Silver-plated Spoon; The Reprint Society Ltd, 1960 (originally published by Cassell in 1959)
Kingdon E V; Tavistock Library; Rep Trans Dev Ass Advmt Sci; 78, 1946
Lee (ed); Dictionary of National Biography, 1900
Lipscombe G; A Journey into Cornwall, 1799
Mettler A E; The Bedford Hotel Tavistock – A Short History; privately published 1986
Mettler A E and Woodcock G; We Will Remember Them – The Men of Tavistock who Died in the First World War; Tavistock and District Local History Society, 2003
Mettler A E and Woodcock G; Lest we Forget – The Tavistock Fallen of the Second World War; Tavistock and District Local History Society, 2006
Murray's Handbook for Devon and Cornwall (1859); David and Charles reprint 1971
Passmore A J; Historic Building Recording at the Bedford Hotel, Tavistock, Devon, 2008; Exeter Archaeology Rept 10.51, 2010
RAC Members Handbooks; 1954 to 1964

Radford G H; Tavistock Abbey; Rep Trans Dev Ass Advmt Sci; 46, 1914

Radford G H; Tavistock Abbey; Exeter Dioc Arch Soc; 3rd Series, 1929

Richardson A E; The Old Inns of England; Batsford, London, 4th edition 1942

Rowe Samuel; A Perambulation of the Ancient and Royal Forest of Dartmoor, 1855, Plymouth

Sournia J C; A History of Alcoholism; Blackwell, Oxford, 1990

Spencer G; Handbook for Tavistock and the neighbourhood; Tavistock, 1860

Trollope A; The Three Clerks, 1858

Vanstone T; Reminiscences of Events Chiefly Connected with Tavistock, 1916; *Tavistock Gazette*

Webb S and B; History of Liquor Licensing in England Principally from 1700 to 1730; Cass and Co, 1963

Woodcock G; Tavistock School – The First Thousand Years; London, 1978

Woodcock G; The Portraits in Tavistock Town Hall, 1988; published by Tavistock Town Council

Woodcock G; A History of Tavistock Cricket Club 1849-1999; Northcote House, Plymouth, 1999

Woodcock G; Tavistock's Yesterdays nos 1-19; privately published, 1985 to 2010, various articles

Trade Directories

Bailey's Western, Midland and London Directory, 1783

Bennett's Directory, 1888

Billing's Directory, 1857

Brindley's Plymouth Directory, 1830

Britton and Brayley's Devonshire and Cornwall Illustrated, 1832

Deacon's Directory, 1882

Eyre's Swiss and Co Plymouth Directories, 1893 to 1932

Flintoff's Plymouth Directory, 1844

White's Directory of Devon, 1850

Harrison and Harrod Directory, 1862

Harrod's Directory, 1878

Holden's Directory, 1811

Kelly's Plymouth Directory, 1937 to 1939

Kelly's Directories for Devon, 1866 to 1939

Morris' Directory for Devonshire, 1870

Pigot's Directories, 1823 to 1852

Robson's Directory, 1840

Rowe's Directory of Plymouth 1814

Smith and Co's Directory, 1867

Taperell's Directory for Plymouth, Dock, Morice Town and Stoke, 1823

Universal British Directory, 1798

White's Directories for Devon, 1850 to 1890

Index

NB – Individual indexed items may appear more than once on any page referred to

Places (except Tavistock)
see also Tavistock places